SEEDS

SEEDS

Thomas Merton

Edited with an introduction by
ROBERT INCHAUSTI

SHAMBHALA
Boston & London
2002

SHAMBHALA PUBLICATIONS, INC.

HORTICULTURAL HALL

300 MASSACHUSETTS AVENUE

BOSTON, MA 02115

www.shambhala.com

9   8   7   6   5   4   3   2   1

First Edition
Printed in the United States of America

♾ This edition is printed on acid-free paper that meets the American
National Standards Institute z39.48 Standard.
Distributed in the United States by Random House, Inc., and
in Canada by Random House of Canada Ltd

Library of Congress Cataloging-in-Publication Data
Merton, Thomas, 1915–1968.
Seeds/Thomas Merton; edited with an introduction by Robert Inchausti.
p.   cm.
ISBN 1-57062-930-7
1. Spiritual life—Catholic Church. I. Inchausti, Robert, 1952–   II.
Title.
BX2350.3 .M47 2002
242—dc21
2002005362

For Linda

The purpose of a book of meditations is to teach you how to think and not to do your thinking for you. Consequently if you pick up such a book and simply read it through, you are wasting your time. As soon as any thought stimulates your mind or your heart you can put the book down because your meditation has begun. To think that you are somehow obliged to follow the author of the book to his own particular conclusion would be a great mistake. It may happen that his conclusion does not apply to you. God may want you to end up somewhere else. He may have planned to give you quite a different grace than the one the author suggests you might be needing.

—*New Seeds of Contemplation*

This is not the official voice of Trappist silence, the monk with his hood up and his back to the camera, brooding over the waters of an artificial lake. This is not the petulant and uncanonizable modern Jerome who never got over the fact that he could give up beer. (I drink beer whenever I can lay my hands on any. I love beer, and by that very fact, the world.) This is simply the voice of a self-questioning human person who, like all his brothers, struggles to cope with turbulent, mysterious, demanding, exciting, frustrating, confused existence in which almost nothing is really predictable, in which most definitions, explanations and justifications become incredible even before they are uttered, in which people suffer together and are sometimes utterly beautiful, at other times impossibly pathetic. In which there is much that is frightening, in which almost everything public is patently phony, and in which there is at the same time an immense ground of personal authenticity that is right there and so obvious that no one can talk about it and most cannot even believe that it is there.

—*Contemplation in a World of Action*

If I dare, in these few words, to ask you some direct and personal questions, it is because I address them as much to myself as to you. It is because I am still able to hope that a civil exchange of ideas can take place between two persons—that we have not yet reached the stage where we are all hermetically sealed, each one in the collective arrogance and despair of his own herd. If I seem to be in a hurry to take advantage of the situation that still exists, it is, frankly, because I sometimes feel it may not continue to exist much longer. In any case, I believe that we are still sufficiently "persons" to realize we have a common difficulty, and to try to solve it together.

—Raids on the Unspeakable

CONTENTS

INTRODUCTION

Thomas Merton was the quintessential American outsider, who defined himself in opposition to the world in both word and deed and then discovered a way back into dialogue with it and compassion for it. He was not a spokesman for any particular group, cause, or idea, but rather the harbinger of a still yet to be realized contemplative counterculture—offering us a vision of an interior life free from rigid philosophical categories, narrow political agendas, and trite religious truisms.

Merton's early years reflected many of the collective experiences of twentieth-century life—loss, loneliness, and lack of meaning. He was born in 1915 in Prades, France, not far from the killing fields of World War I. The war forced his financially struggling ex-patriot parents to return to New York, where, six years later, his mother died of stomach cancer. Merton spent the rest of his childhood with his father, an aspiring watercolorist, traveling back and forth from the United States to Europe. He attended P.S. 98 in Douglaston, New York, the French Lycée at Montauban, and the Oakham prep school in England. In 1931 his father died of a brain tumor.

Two years later Merton entered Clare College, Cambridge, intending to pursue a career in diplomacy, but he actually spent most of his time going to parties and "indulging his appetites," as he wrote later. He lost his scholarship and got kicked out of the university for, among other things, fathering a child out of wedlock and participating in a drunken fraternity party, where, according to accounts, he was ritually crucified.

Merton returned to New York the next year and tried to shape up by joining the Communist Party. He took the so-called "Oxford Pledge" never to fight in any wars and participated in street protests against the war in Ethiopia. But though political radicalism gave his life the semblance of an ethical order, Merton was still morally and philosophically at sea amid the torrential instabilities of the thirties.

Slowly, however, he began to meet the men who would help him find himself. He studied with Mark Van Doren, a Pulitzer Prize–winning poet and critic, and with Joseph Wood Krutch, a naturalist and environmentalist whose numerous books included *The Modern Temper* (1929) and a celebrated biography of Henry David Thoreau. Merton's circle of friends also grew to include the likes of Ad Reinhardt, who went on to become a famous abstract expressionist and minimalist painter, and Robert Lax, the celebrated avant-garde poet.

Inspired, Merton threw himself into his studies. Under Mark Van Doren's tutelage, he began reading for inspiration and spiritual illumination, searching for ideas he could experience and apply to his life rather than for mere historical and theoretical knowledge. He also joined the staff of the *Columbia Jester*, began writing a novel, and developed an interest in Eastern religions. One of his professors, a Hindu monk named Bramachari, suggested that he read the Western spiritual writers before studying the Eastern ones, and Merton never fully recovered from this suggestion. He read so deeply in the Western spiritual tradition that he was transformed from the inside out—converting to Catholicism two years later.

The dramatic turning point in Merton's life, however, didn't occur until April 1941. Although he had been studying Catholicism for several years and was thinking about becoming a priest, it wasn't until he visited the Abbey of Gethsemani that he discovered—in that peaceful, physically demanding community of cloistered monks—the alternative life he was looking for. That day he wrote in his journal,

> I should tear out all the other pages of this book, and all the other pages of anything else I've ever written, and begin here.
>
> This is the center of America. I had wondered what was holding the country together, what had been keeping the universe from cracking to pieces and falling apart. . . .This is the only real city in America—and it is by itself in the wilderness. It is an axle around which the whole country blindly turns and

knows nothing about it. Gethsemani holds the country together
the way the underlying substrata of natural faith that goes with
our whole being and can hardly be separated from it, keeps
living on in a man who has "lost his faith"—who no longer
believes in Being and yet himself *is*, in spite of his crazy denial
that he Who IS mercifully allowed him to *be*.   (sj 183–84*)

Merton decided then and there to enter the monastery (if the Trappists
would have him), thus sealing his shift in allegiance from the secular lite-
rati with "their 'no' to everything that served as their pitiful 'yes' to themselves" to a life of contemplation in a religious community where time and
transcendence merged in the holy present and grace fell as "gratuitous as
rain."

His reasoning was really very simple: If bourgeois civilization was fail-
ing, then leave it; if the West had become blind to its spiritual heritage,
then reclaim it; and if poverty and obscurity were the price one had to
pay to live a life in accord with conscience, then wholeheartedly embrace
them and don't look back.

Merton's decision to "leave the world" was really an extension of his
new "examined" life. By entering the monastery, he was not only turning
his back on the entire materialist and positivist thrust of contemporary
civilization, but also questioning the effectiveness of the artistic counterculture and political radicalism that pretended to scorn it. Yet Merton
never thought of his decision to enter a monastery as a rejection of the
world so much as a refusal to participate in lies and support false actions.

As far as I can see, what I abandoned when I "left the world"
and came to the monastery was the *understanding of myself*
that I had developed in the context of civil society—my identification with what appeared to me to be its aims. Certainly, in
the concrete, "the world" did not mean for me either riches (I
was poor) or a life of luxury, certainly not the ambition to get

*For a key to the abbreviations of Merton titles, see the Sources and Abbreviations section.

somewhere in business or in anything else except writing. But it did mean a certain set of servitudes that I could no longer accept—servitudes to certain standards of value which to me were idiotic and repugnant and still are. Many of these were trivial, some of them were onerous, all are closely related. The image of a society that is happy because it drinks Coca-Cola or Seagrams or both and is protected by the bomb. The society that is imaged in the mass media and in advertising, in the movies, in TV, in best-sellers, in current fads, in all the pompous and trifling masks with which it hides callousness, sensuality, hypocrisy, cruelty, and fear. (CGB 36)

After entering the order, Merton immersed himself even more deeply in monastic tradition. He gave up writing fiction for poetry, saints' lives, and ecclesiastical history. Under orders from the abbot, he wrote a spiritual autobiography that told the story of his transformation from skeptic to Trappist contemplative. *The Seven Storey Mountain* was published in 1948, shortly after the worst war in human history. The nuclear arms race was just beginning, and the civil rights movement was raising disturbing questions about America's commitment to democratic values. Merton's soul-searching autobiography offered a vision of life that transcended these confusions through an overt and complete rejection of the materialistic aspirations and moral compromises of contemporary civilization. To everyone's surprise, it became an international best-seller, catapulting him from the obscurity of his "silent life" into instant celebrity.

As the fifties progressed, Merton was deeply moved by Catholic peace activist Dorothy Day's refusal to participate in civil defense drills and by Martin Luther King's courageous nonviolent assault upon race prejudice and inequality. Merton published some of his lectures on contemplation and started to write essays directly addressed to his secular contemporaries. He also began a series of correspondences with a variety of thinkers that included the neo-Marxist Eric Fromm, the Buddhist scholar D. T. Suzuki, the Nobel laureate poet and critic of totalitarianism Czeslaw Milosz, and the Jewish scholar, mystic, and activist Abraham Heschel.

After the Cuban missile crisis had brought the world to the threshold of nuclear annihilation in 1962, the United States experienced a succession of political horrors that included the Kennedy assassination; the Watts, Detroit, and Washington, D.C., riots; and the escalating war in Vietnam. These events brought into question the existing social order, giving rise to public protests and disaffection among minorities and the young. As a result, Merton's reflections on the spiritual poverty of contemporary life began to take on a new social relevance. The controversial satirist Lenny Bruce began to read Merton's poetry in his nightclub act, and even the Black Power revolutionary Eldridge Cleaver quoted him at length in his controversial autobiography, *Soul on Ice.*

Meanwhile, Merton was reading Franz Fanon's *Black Skin, White Masks*, Herbert Marcuse's *One-Dimensional Man*, and Jacques Ellul's *The Technological Society.* Writing to James Forest, a war protester and member of Dorothy Day's Catholic Worker community, Merton succinctly summed up his take on all these books and developments:

> It seems to me that the most basic problem is not political, it is apolitical and human. One of the most important things to do is to keep cutting deliberately through political lines and barriers and emphasizing the fact that these are largely fabrications and that there is another dimension, a genuine reality, totally opposed to the fictions of politics, the human dimension which politicians pretend to arrogate entirely to themselves. . . . Is this possible? (HGL 272)

Merton spent the rest of his life trying to prove that it was indeed possible and attempting to give voice to this "genuine reality."

Collected here are some of the fruits of his efforts. The selections are organized in four parts, which to some extent parallel Merton's own development: Part One attempts to draw the distinction between our false and true selves, between the pseudo-identities we possess as conditioned members of society and the persons we truly are, known only by God. Part Two presents Merton's view of the state of the modern world as "a deep elemental boiling over of all the inner contradictions that have ever been in man." Part Three focuses on his antidotes to cultural illusion, while Part Four explores the existential difficulties that emerge once one truly begins to engage in the struggle for justice and true sanctification.

This four-part structure somewhat belies the cyclical and improvisational nature of much of Merton's writing. He was never really a problem solver *per se*, and he seldom attempted to lay down the law theologically. His method, insofar as he can be said to have one, was far more personal, informal, and tentative: literary and phenomenological. He was, if you will, an explorer on the frontiers of human self-understanding—testing ideas out with his own life, coming back to them again and again to resolve certain ambiguities and refine his ideas—all the while creating within himself an ever more inclusive map of the cosmos. And although Merton never challenged the essential message of Christianity, he did rediscover truths we seemed to have lost and put them in new contexts by which they could be more fully appreciated and understood.

I have collected paragraphs here—as opposed to essays—partly because it is the most succinct way to introduce Merton's ideas, but more importantly because the paragraph was Merton's literary strength. He thought and composed in paragraphs that modeled his own reflective thought processes: single ideas growing thematically, lyrically, and dialectically out of themselves, making unexpected connections, and then emerging into surprising new epiphanies. If the rhetoric of Merton's longer works can sometimes be formidable, his paragraphs are always accessible, poignant, and revelatory.

Merton died by accidental electrocution while attending an international conference on monasticism in Bangkok, Thailand, in 1968, the very same year Martin Luther King, Jr., and Robert F. Kennedy were assassinated. His trip to the East had included meetings with the Dalai Lama and Thich Nhat Hanh—the celebrated Vietnamese Zen Master who was nominated for a Nobel Prize by Martin Luther King and continues to teach meditation to this day. Merton's early death cut short his conversation with the East and silenced one of the twentieth-century's most creative and ecumenical thinkers.

Merton described his life's work this way:

> My own peculiar task in my Church and in my world has been that of the solitary explorer who, instead of jumping on all the latest bandwagons at once, is bound to search the existential depths of faith in its silences, its ambiguities, and in those certainties which lie deeper than the bottom of anxiety. In those depths there are no easy answers, no pat solutions to anything. It is a kind of submarine life in which faith sometimes mysteriously takes on the aspect of doubt, when, in fact, one has to doubt and reject conventional and superstitious surrogates that have taken the place of faith. (FAV 213)

By exposing the "conventional and superstitious surrogates" for faith, Thomas Merton taught us what it means to live a life of conscience in difficult times. He combined the rigor of the New York intellectuals with the probity of the Desert Fathers—speaking directly to our solitude through a rigorous examination of his own. By so doing, he closed the gap between our exterior, social selves and our interior, undetermined freedom. When we read his works, we have the strange sensation of being both found out and set free. For although he undermines our illusory ambitions, questions our values, and assaults our complacency, he also gives solace to our impoverished souls by reminding us of a larger, more inclusive, transcendent reality of which we are all a part.

ROBERT INCHAUSTI
San Luis Obispo, California

PART ONE

Real and False Selves

At the heart of Merton's spirituality is his distinction between our real and false selves. Our false selves are the
identities we cultivate in order to function in society with
pride and self-possession; our real selves are a deep religious mystery, known entirely only to God. The world
cultivates the false self, ignores the real one, and therein
lies the great irony of human existence: The more we
make of ourselves, the less we actually exist.

All sin starts from the assumption that my false self, the self that exists only in my own egocentric desires, is the fundamental reality of life to which everything else in the universe is ordered. Thus I use up my life in the desire for pleasures and the thirst for experiences, for power, honor, knowledge, and love to clothe this false self and construct its nothingness into something objectively real. And I wind experiences around myself and cover myself with pleasures and glory like bandages in order to make myself perceptible to myself and to the world, as if I were an invisible body that could only become visible when something visible covered its surface.

(NS 34–35)

◆ ◆ ◆

If we take our vulnerable shell to be our true identity, if we think our mask is our true face, we will protect it with fabrications even at the cost of violating our own truth. This seems to be the collective endeavor of society: the more busily men dedicate themselves to it, the more certainly it becomes a collective illusion, until in the end we have the enormous, obsessive, uncontrollable dynamic of fabrications designed to protect mere fictitious identities—"selves," that is to say, regarded as objects. Selves that can stand back and see themselves having fun (an illusion which reassures them that they are real).

(RU 15)

◆ ◆ ◆

To say I was born in sin is to say I came into the world with a false self. I was born in a mask. I came into existence under a sign of contradiction, being someone that I was never intended to be and therefore a denial of what I am supposed to be. And thus I came into existence and nonexistence at the same time because from the very start I was something that I was not. (NS 33–34)

◆ ◆ ◆

The deep secrecy of my own being is often hidden from me by my own estimate of what I am. My idea of what I am is falsified by my admiration for what I do. And my illusions about myself are bred by contagion from the illusions of other men. We all seek to imitate one another's imagined greatness.

If I do not know who I am, it is because I think I am the sort of person everyone around me wants to be. Perhaps I have never asked myself whether I really wanted to become what everybody else seems to want to become. Perhaps if I only realized that I do not admire what everyone seems to admire, I would really begin to live after all. I would be liberated from the painful duty of saying what I really do not think and acting in a way that betrays God's truth and the integrity of my own soul. (NM 125–26)

◆ ◆ ◆

When a man constantly looks and looks at himself in the mirror of his own acts, his spiritual double vision splits him into two people. And if he strains his eyes hard enough, he forgets which one is real. In fact, reality is no longer found either in himself or in his shadow. The substance has gone out of itself into the shadow, and he has become two shadows instead of one real person.

Then the battle begins. Whereas one shadow was meant to praise the other, now one shadow accuses the other. The activity that was meant to exalt him, reproaches and condemns him. It is never real enough. Never active enough. The less he is able to *be* the more he has to *do*. He becomes his own slave driver—a shadow whipping a shadow to death, because it cannot produce reality, infinitely substantial reality, out of his own nonentity. (NM 119)

◆ ◆ ◆

Every one of us is shadowed by an illusory person: a false self.

This is the man that I want to be but who cannot exist, because God does not know anything about him. And to be unknown of God is altogether too much privacy. (NS 34)

◆ ◆ ◆

In order to experience your [false] self as real, you have to suppress the awareness of your contingency, your unreality, your state of radical need. This you do by creating an awareness of yourself as *one who has no needs that he cannot immediately fulfill*. Basically, this is an illusion of omnipotence: an illusion which the collectivity arrogates to itself, and consents to share with its individual members in proportion as they submit to its more central and more rigid fabrications.

You have needs; but if you behave and conform you can participate in the collective power. You can then satisfy all your needs. Meanwhile, in order to increase its power over you, the collectivity increases your needs. It also tightens its demand for conformity. Thus you can become all the more committed to the collective illusion in proportion to becoming more hopelessly mortgaged to collective power.

How does this work? The collectivity informs and shapes your will to happiness ("have fun") by presenting you with irresistible images of yourself as you would like to be: having *fun that is so perfectly credible that it allows no interference of conscious doubt.* In theory such a good time can be so convincing that you are no longer aware of even a remote possibility that it might change into something less satisfying. In practice, expensive fun always admits of a doubt, which blossoms out into another full-blown need, which then calls for a still more credible and more costly refinement of satisfaction, which again fails you. The end of the cycle is despair.

(RU 15–16)

◆ ◆ ◆

The man who lives in division is not a person but only an "individual."

I have what you have not. I am what you are not. I have taken what you have failed to take and I have seized what you could never get. Therefore you suffer and I am happy, you are despised and I am praised, you die and I live; you are nothing and I am something, and I am all the more something because you are nothing. And thus I spend my life admiring the distance between you and me; at times this even helps me to forget the other men who have what I have not and who have taken what I was too slow to take and who have seized what was beyond my reach, who are praised as I cannot be praised and who live on my death. . . .

The man who lives in division is living in death. He cannot find himself because he is lost; he has ceased to be a reality. The person he believes himself to be is a bad dream. And when he dies he will discover that he long ago ceased to exist because God, Who is infinite reality and in Whose sight is the being of everything that is, will say to him: "I know you not."

(NS 48)

◆ ◆ ◆

The earthly desires men cherish are shadows. There is no true happiness in fulfilling them. Why, then, do we continue to pursue joys without substance? Because the pursuit itself has become our only substitute for joy. Unable to rest in anything we achieve, we determine to forget our discontent in a ceaseless quest for new satisfactions. In this pursuit, desire itself becomes our chief satisfaction.

(ATT 17)

◆ ◆ ◆

There is a paradox that lies in the very heart of human existence. It must be apprehended before any lasting happiness is possible in the soul of a man. The paradox is this: man's nature, by itself, can do little or nothing to settle his most important problems. If we follow nothing but our natures, our own philosophies, our own level of ethics, we will end up in hell.

This would be a depressing thought, if it were not purely abstract. Because in the concrete order of things God gave man a nature that was ordered to a supernatural life. He created man with a soul that was made not to bring itself to perfection in its own order, but to be perfected by Him in an order infinitely beyond the reach of human powers. We were never destined to lead purely natural lives, and therefore we were never destined in God's plan for a purely natural beatitude. Our nature, which is a free gift of God, was given us to be perfected and enhanced by another free gift that is not due it.

(SSM 169)

◆ ◆ ◆

To start with one's ego-identity and to try to bring that identity to terms with external reality by thinking, and then, having worked out practical principles, to act on reality from one privileged autonomous position—in order to bring it into line with an absolute good we have arrived at by thought: this is the way we become irresponsible. If reality is something we interpret and act on to suit our own concept of ourselves, we "respond" to nothing. We simply dictate our own terms, and "realism" consists in keeping the terms somewhat plausible. But this implies no real respect for reality, for other persons, for their needs, and in the end it implies no real respect for ourselves, since, without bothering to question the deep mystery of our own identity, we fabricate a trifling and impertinent identity for ourselves with the bare scraps of experience that we find lying within immediate reach. (CGB 242)

◆ ◆ ◆

To assume that my superficial ego—this cramp of the imagination—is my real self is to begin by dishonoring myself and reality. Then I am left with a choice between a servile adjustment that submits to facts and manipulates my ego-concept to defend it against subversion by the facts, or else a rebellious attitude which denies the facts and tries to flout them, again in the interests of the ego-image.

"Adjustment" becomes a constant play of "yes" and "no," an organized system of ambivalences, circling around one central ambivalence—a relative and contingent ego-image trying to constitute itself as an absolute. Here what we first intend *as* an absolute "yes" becomes inexorably an absolute "no." But our life continues as a more and more desperate struggle to keep ourselves in focus as an *affirmation* not as a *negation*.

Such a project is simply and utterly futile.

We must go back to the beginning. What beginning? The beginning of our thought? Or the real beginning which we cannot reach, which is too close to ourselves to be seen? How can we ever "go back" to it? Back where? The beginning is *now*.   (CGB 242–43)

◆ ◆ ◆

The tragedy of a life centered on "things," on the grasping and manipulation of objects, is that such a life closes the ego upon itself as though it were an end in itself, and throws it into a hopeless struggle with other perverse and hostile selves competing together for the possessions which will give them power and satisfaction. Instead of being "open to the world" such minds are in fact closed to it and their titanic efforts to build the world according to their own desires are doomed in the end by the ambiguity and destructiveness that are in them. They seem to be light, but they battle together in impenetrable moral darkness.   (Z&B 82)

◆ ◆ ◆

If we want to understand alienation, we have to find where its deepest taproot goes—and we have to realize that this root will always be there. Alienation is inseparable from culture, from civilization, and from life in society. It is not just a feature of "bad" cultures, "corrupt" civilizations, or urban society. It is not just a dubious privilege reserved for some people in society. . . . Alienation begins when culture divides me against myself, puts a mask on me, gives me a role I may or may not want to play. Alienation is complete when I become completely identified with my mask, totally satisfied with my role, and convince myself that any other identity or role is inconceivable. The man who sweats under his mask, whose role makes him itch with discomfort, who hates the division in himself, is already beginning to be free. But God help him if all he wants is the mask the other man is wearing, just because the other one does not seem to be sweating or itching. Maybe he is no longer human enough to itch. (Or else he pays a psychiatrist to scratch him.)

(LE 381)

◆ ◆ ◆

The way to find the real "world" is not merely to measure and observe what is outside us, but to discover our own inner ground. For that is where the world is, first of all: in my deepest self. This "ground," this "world" where I am mysteriously present at once to my own self and to the freedoms of all other men, is not a visible, objective and determined structure with fixed laws and demands. It is a living and self-creating mystery of which I am myself a part, to which I am myself my own unique door.   (CIWA 154–55)

◆ ◆ ◆

The shallow "I" of individualism can be possessed, developed, cultivated, and pandered to, satisfied: it is the center of all our strivings for gains and for satisfaction, whether material or spiritual. But the deep "I" of the spirit, of solitude and of love, cannot be "had," possessed, developed, perfected. It can only be and act according to the inner laws which are not of man's contriving but which come from God. They are the Laws of the Spirit who, like the wind, blows where He wills. This inner "I," who is always alone, is always universal: for in this most inmost "I" my own solitude meets the solitude of every other man and the solitude of God. Hence it is beyond division, beyond limitation, beyond selfish affirmation.

(DQ 207)

◆ ◆ ◆

The more one seeks "the good" outside oneself as something to be acquired, the more one is faced with the necessity of discussing, studying, understanding, analyzing the nature of the good. The more, therefore, one becomes involved in abstractions and in the confusion of divergent opinions. The more "the good" is objectively analyzed, the more it is treated as something to be attained by special virtuous techniques, the less real it becomes. As it becomes less real, it recedes further into the distance of abstraction, futurity, unattainability. The more, therefore, one concentrates on the means to be used to attain it. And as the end becomes more remote and more difficult, the means become more elaborate and complex, until finally the mere study of the means becomes so demanding that all one's effort must be concentrated on this, and the end is forgotten.

(woc 23)

◆   ◆   ◆

There is and can be no special planned technique for discovering and awakening one's inner self, because the inner self is first of all a spontaneity that is nothing if not free. Therefore there is no use in trying to start with a definition of the inner self, and then deducing from its essential properties some appropriate and infallible means of submitting it to control—as if the essence could give us some clue to that which is vulnerable in it, something we can lay hold of, in order to gain power over it. Such an idea would imply a complete misapprehension of the existential reality we are talking about. The inner self is not a part of our being, like a motor in a car. It is our entire substantial reality itself, on its highest and most personal and most existential level. It is like life, and it is life: it is our spiritual life when it is most alive. It is the life by which everything else in us lives and moves. It is in and through and beyond everything that we are. If it is awakened it communicates a new life to the intelligence in which it lives, so that it becomes a living awareness of itself: and this awareness is not so much something that we ourselves have, as something that we are. It is a new and indefinable quality of our living being.

The inner self is as secret as God and, like Him, it evades every concept that tries to seize hold of it with full possession. It is a life that cannot be held and studied as object, because it is not "a thing." It is not reached and coaxed forth from hiding by any process under the sun, including meditation. All that we can do with any spiritual discipline is produce within ourselves something of the silence, the humility, the detachment, the purity of heart and the indifference which are required if the inner self is to make some shy, unpredictable manifestation of his Presence. (CQR 5–6)

◆　◆　◆

We do not have to create a conscience for ourselves. We are born with one, and no matter how much we may ignore it, we cannot silence its insistent demand that we do good and avoid evil. No matter how much we may deny our freedom and our moral responsibility, our intellectual soul cries out for a morality and a spiritual freedom without which it knows it cannot be happy. (NM 41–42)

◆　◆　◆

In our being there is a primordial *yes* that is not our own; it is not at our own disposal; it is not accessible to our inspection and understanding; we do not even fully experience it as real (except in rare and unique circumstances). And we have to admit that for most people this primordial "yes" is something they never advert to at all. It is in fact absolutely unconscious, totally forgotten.

Basically, however, my being is not an affirmation of a limited self, but the "yes" of Being itself, irrespective of my own choices. Where do "I" come in? Simply in uniting the "yes" of my own freedom with the "yes" of Being that already *is* before I have a chance to choose. This is not "adjustment." There is nothing to adjust. There is reality, and there is free consent. There is the actuality of one "yes." In this actuality no question of "adjustment" remains and the ego vanishes. (CGB 243)

◆ ◆ ◆

The root of personality is to be sought in the "true Self" which is manifested in the basic unification of consciousness in which subject and object are one. Hence the highest good is "the self's fusion with the highest reality."* Human personality is regarded as the force which effects this fusion. The hopes and desires of the external, individual self are all, in fact, opposed to this higher unity. They are centered on the affirmation of the individual. It is only at the point where the hopes and fears of the individual self are done away with and forgotten "that the true human personality appears." In a word, realization of the human personality in this highest spiritual sense is for us the good toward which all life is to be oriented. (Z&B 69)

◆ ◆ ◆

The measure of our being is not to be sought in the violence of our experiences. Turbulence of spirit is a sign of spiritual weakness. When delights spring out of our depths like leopards, we have nothing to be proud of: our soul's life is in danger. For when we are strong, we are always much greater than the things that happen to

*This and the following quoted phrase are from *A Study of Good* by Kitaro Nishida (1870–1945), a Japanese philosopher schooled in Zen Buddhism.

us, and the soul of a man who has found himself is like a deep sea in which there may be many fish, but they never come up out of the sea, and not one of them is big enough to trouble its placid surface. His "being" is far greater than anything he feels or does.   (NM 125)

◆ ◆ ◆

Our being is not to be enriched merely by activity and experience as such. Everything depends on the *quality* of our acts and our experiences. A multitude of badly performed actions and of experiences only half-lived exhausts and depletes our being. By doing things badly we make ourselves less real. This growing unreality cannot help but make us unhappy and fill us with a sense of guilt. But the purity of our conscience has a natural proportion with the depth of our being and the quality of our acts: and when our activity is habitually disordered, our malformed conscience can think of nothing better to tell us than to multiply the *quantity* of our acts, without perfecting their quality. And so we go from bad to worse, exhaust ourselves, empty our whole life of all content, and fall into despair.

There are times, then, when in order to keep ourselves in existence at all we simply have to sit back for a while and do nothing. And for a man who has let himself be drawn completely out of himself by his activity, nothing is more difficult than to sit still and rest, doing nothing at all. The very act of resting is the hardest and most courageous act he can perform: and often it is quite beyond his power.

We must first recover the possession of our own being. (NM 123)

◆ ◆ ◆

One of the most important—and most neglected—elements in the beginnings of the interior life is the ability to respond to reality, to see the value and the beauty in ordinary things, to come alive to the splendor that is all around us in the creatures of God. We do not see these things because we have withdrawn from them. In a way we have to. In modern life our senses are so constantly bombarded with stimulation from every side that unless we developed a kind of protective insensibility we would go crazy trying to respond to *all* the advertisements at the same time!

The first step in the interior life, nowadays, is not, as some might imagine, learning *not* to see and taste and hear and feel things. On the contrary, what we must do is begin by unlearning our wrong ways of seeing, tasting, feeling, and so forth, and acquire a few of the right ones.

For asceticism is not merely a matter of renouncing television, cigarettes, and gin. Before we can begin to be ascetics, we first have to learn to see life as if it were something more than a hypnotizing telecast. And we must be able to taste something besides tobacco and alcohol: we must perhaps even be able to taste these luxuries themselves as if they too were good.

How can our conscience tell us whether or not we are renouncing things unless it first tells us that how to use them properly? For renunciation is not an end in itself: it helps us to use things better. It helps us to give them away. If reality revolts us, if we merely turn away from it in disgust, to whom shall we sacrifice it? How shall we consecrate it? How shall we make of it a gift to God and to men?

(NM 33–34)

◆ ◆ ◆

True solitude is found in humility, which is infinitely rich. False solitude is the refuge of pride, and it is infinitely poor. The poverty of false solitude comes from an illusion which pretends, by adorning itself in things it can never possess, to distinguish one individual self from the mass of other men. True solitude is selfless. Therefore, it is rich in silence and charity and peace. It finds in itself seemingly inexhaustible resources of good to bestow on other people. False solitude is self-centered. And because it finds nothing in its own center, it seeks to draw all things into itself. But everything it touches becomes infected with its own nothingness, and falls apart. True solitude cleans the soul, lays it wide open to the four winds of generosity. False solitude locks the door against all men and pores over its own private accumulation of rubbish.

Both solitudes seek to distinguish the individual from the crowd. True solitude succeeds in this; false solitude fails. True solitude separates one man from the rest in order that he may freely develop the good that is his own, and then fulfill his true destiny by putting himself at the service of everyone else. False solitude separates a man from his brothers in such a way that he can no longer effectively give them anything or receive anything from them in his own spirit. It establishes him in a state of indigence, misery, blindness, torment, and despair. Maddened by his own insufficiency, the proud man shamelessly seizes upon satisfactions and possessions that are not due to him, that can never satisfy him, and that he will never really need. Because he has never learned to distinguish what is really his, he desperately seeks to possess what can never belong to him.

(NM 248–49)

◆ ◆ ◆

One of the most widespread errors of our time is a superficial "personalism" which identifies the "person" with the external self, the empirical ego, and devotes itself solemnly to the cultivation of this ego.

But this is the cult of a pure illusion, the illusion of what is popularly imagined to be "personality" or worse still "dynamic" and "successful" personality. When this error is taken over into religion it leads to the worst kind of nonsense—a cult of psychologism and self-expression which vitiates our whole cultural and spiritual self. Our reality, our true self, is hidden in what appears to us to be nothingness and void. What we are not seems to be real, what we are seems to be unreal. We can rise above this unreality, and recover our hidden identity. And that is why the way to reality is the way of humility which brings us to reject the illusory self and accept the "empty" self that is "nothing" in our own eyes and in the eyes of men, but is our true reality in the eyes of God: for this reality is "in God" and "with Him" and belongs entirely to Him. Yet of course it is ontologically distinct from Him and in no sense part of the divine nature or absorbed in that nature.

This inmost self is beyond the kind of experience which says "I want," "I love," "I know," "I feel." It has its own way of knowing, loving, and experiencing which is a divine way and not a human one, a way of identity, of union, of "espousal," in which there is no longer a separate psychological individuality drawing all good and truth toward itself, and thus loving and knowing for itself. Lover and Beloved are "one spirit."

Therefore, as long as we experience ourselves in prayer as an "I" standing on the threshold of the abyss of purity and emptiness that is God, waiting to "receive something" from Him, we are still far from the most intimate and secretive union that is pure contemplation.

From our side of the threshold this darkness, this emptiness, looks deep and vast—and exciting. There is nothing we can do about entering it. We cannot force our way over the edge, although there is no barrier.

But the reason is perhaps that there is also no abyss.

There you remain, somehow feeling that the next step will be a plunge and you will find yourself flying in interstellar space.

(NS 281–82)

❖ ❖ ❖

It is not complicated to lead the spiritual life. But it is difficult. We are blind, and subject to a thousand illusions. We must expect to be making mistakes almost all the time. We must be content to fall repeatedly and to begin again to try to deny ourselves, for the love of God.

It is when we are angry at our own mistakes that we tend most of all to deny ourselves for love of ourselves. We want to shake off the hateful thing that has humbled us. In our rush to escape the humiliation of our own mistakes, we run head first into the opposite error, seeking comfort and compensation. And so we spend our lives running back and forth from one attachment to another.

If that is all our self-denial amounts to, our mistakes will never help us.

The thing to do when you have made a mistake is not to give up doing what you were doing and start something altogether new, but to start over again with the thing you began badly and try, for the love of God, to do it well.   (soj 242)

❖ ❖ ❖

Many of the problems and sufferings of the spiritual life today are either fictitious or they should not have to be put up with. But because of our mentality we block the "total response" that is needed for a fully healthy and fruitful spirituality. In fact the very idea of "spirituality" tends to be unhealthy in so far as it is divisive and itself makes total response impossible. The "spiritual" life thus becomes something to be lived "interiorly" and in "the spirit" (or worse still in the "mind"—indeed in the "imagination"). The body is left out of it, because the body is "bad" or at best "unspiritual.". . .

So we create problems that should never arise, simply because we "believe" with our mind, but heart and body do not follow. Or else the heart and the emotions drive on in some direction of their own, with the mind in total confusion. The damnable abstractness of the "spiritual life" in this sense is ruining people. . . . All is reduced to "intentions" and "interior acts," and one is instructed to "purify one's intention" and bear the Cross mentally, while physically and psychologically one is more and more deeply involved in an over-worked, unbalanced, irrational, even inhuman existence.

(CGB 253–54)

◆ ◆ ◆

The things we really need come to us only as gifts, and in order to receive them as gifts we have to be open. In order to be open we have to renounce ourselves, in a sense we have to *die* to our image of ourselves, our autonomy, our fixation upon our self-willed iden-tity. We have to be able to relax the psychic and spiritual cramp which knots us in the painful, vulnerable, helpless "I" that is all we know as ourselves.

The chronic inability to relax this cramp begets despair. In the end, as we realize more and more that we are knotted upon *nothing*, that the cramp is a meaningless, senseless, pointless affirmation of nonentity, and that we must nevertheless continue to affirm our nothingness *over against* everything else—our frustration becomes absolute. We become incapable of existing except as a "no," which we fling in the face of everything. This "no" to everything serves as our pitiful "yes" to ourselves—a makeshift identity which is nothing.

(CGB 204)

◆ ◆ ◆

The heresy of individualism: thinking oneself a completely self-sufficient unit and asserting this imaginary "unity" against all others. The affirmation of the self as simply "not the other." But when you seek to affirm your unity by denying that you have anything to do with anyone else, by negating everyone else in the universe until you come down to *you:* what is there left to affirm? Even if there were something to affirm, you would have no breath left with which to affirm it.

The true way is just the opposite: the more I am able to affirm others, to say "yes" to them in myself, by discovering them in myself and myself in them, the more real I am. I am fully real if my own heart says *yes* to *everyone.*

I will be a better Catholic, not if I can *refute* every shade of Protestantism, but if I can affirm the truth in it and still go further.

So, too, with the Muslims, the Hindus, the Buddhists, etc. This does not mean syncretism, indifferentism, the vapid and careless friendliness that accepts everything by thinking of nothing. There is much that one cannot "affirm" and "accept," but first one must say "yes" where one really can.

If I affirm myself as a Catholic merely by denying all that is Muslim, Jewish, Protestant, Hindu, Buddhist, etc., in the end I will find that there is not much left for me to affirm as a Catholic: and certainly no breath of the Spirit with which to affirm it. (CGB 128–29)

◆　◆　◆

We ought to have the humility to admit we do not know all about ourselves, that we are not experts at running our own lives. We ought to stop taking our conscious plans and decisions with such infinite seriousness. It may well be that we are *not* the martyrs or the mystics or the apostles or the leaders or the lovers of God that we imagine ourselves to be. Our subconscious mind may be trying to tell us this in many ways—and we have trained ourselves, with the most egregious self-righteousness to turn a deaf ear.   (NM 38)

◆ ◆ ◆

The problem is to learn how to renounce resentment without selling out to the organization people who want everyone to accept absurdity and moral anarchy in a spirit of uplift and willing complicity. Few men are strong enough to find the solution. A monastery is not necessarily the right answer; there is resentment in monasteries also, and for the same reason that there is resentment anywhere else.

If you want to renounce resentment, you have to renounce the shadow self that feels itself menaced by the confusion without which it cannot subsist. This is the problem: having to live in complete servile dependence upon a system, an organization, a society, or a person that one despises or hates. To live in such dependence and yet to be compelled, by one's own attachment to what appears to be an "identity," to seemingly approve and accept what one hates. To have an "I" that is essentially servile and dependent, and which expresses its servility by constantly lauding and flattering the tyrant to whom it remains unwillingly, yet necessarily, subject.   (NS 109)

◆ ◆ ◆

To live well myself is my first and essential contribution to the well-being of all mankind and to the fulfillment of man's collective destiny. If I do not live happily myself how can I help anyone else to be happy, or free, or wise? Yet to seek happiness is not to live happily. Perhaps it is more true to say that one finds happiness by not seeking it. The wisdom that teaches us deliberately to restrain our desire for happiness enables us to discover that we are already happy without realizing the fact.

To live well myself means for me to know and appreciate something of the secret, the mystery in myself: that which is incommunicable, which is at once myself and not myself, at once in me and above me. From this sanctuary I must seek humbly and patiently to ward off all the intrusions of violence and self-assertion. These intrusions cannot really penetrate the sanctuary, but they can draw me forth from it and slay me before the secret doorway.

If I can understand something of myself and something of others, I can begin to share with them the work of building the foundations for spiritual unity. But first we must work together at dissipating the more absurd fictions which make unity impossible.   (CGB 81–82)

◆   ◆   ◆

He who is spiritually "born" as a mature identity is liberated from the enclosing womb of myth and prejudice. He learns to think for himself, guided no longer by the dictates of need and by the systems and processes designed to create artificial needs and then "satisfy" them.

This emancipation can take two forms: first that of the active life, which liberates itself from enslavement to necessity by considering and serving the needs of others, without thought of personal interest or return. And second, the contemplative life, which must not be construed as an escape from time and matter, from social responsibility and from the life of sense, but rather, as an advance into solitude and the desert, confrontation with poverty and the void, a renunciation of the empirical self, in the presence of death, and nothingness, in order to overcome the ignorance and error that spring from the fear of being nothing.   (RU 17–18)

◆   ◆   ◆

The only true joy on earth is to escape from the prison of our own false self, and enter by love into union with the Life Who dwells and sings within the essence of every creature and in the core of our own souls. In His love we possess all things and enjoy fruition of them, finding Him in them all. And thus as we go about the world, everything we meet and everything we see and hear and touch, far from defiling, purifies us and plants in us something more of contemplation and of heaven.

Short of this perfection, created things do not bring us joy but pain. Until we love God perfectly, everything in the world will be able to hurt us. And the greatest misfortune is to be dead to the pain they inflict on us, and not to realize what it is.

For until we love God perfectly His world is full of contradiction. The things He has created attract us to Him and yet keep us away from Him. They draw us on and they stop us dead. We find Him in them to some extent and then we don't find Him in them at all.

Just when we think we have discovered some joy in them, the joy turns into sorrow; and just when they are beginning to please us the pleasure turns into pain.

In all created things we, who do not yet perfectly love God, can find something that reflects the fulfillment of heaven and something that reflects the anguish of hell. We find something of the joy of blessedness and something of the pain of loss, which is damnation.

The fulfillment we find in creatures belongs to the reality of the created being, a reality that is from God and belongs to God and reflects God. The anguish we find in them belongs to the disorder of our desire which looks for a greater reality in the object of our desire than is actually there: a greater fulfillment than any created thing is capable of giving. Instead of worshipping God through His creation we are always trying to worship ourselves by means of creatures.   (NS 25–26)

◆　◆　◆

[The] self is not by nature evil, and the fact that it is unsubstantial is not to be imputed to it as some kind of crime. It is afflicted with metaphysical poverty: but all that is poor deserves mercy. So too our outward self: as long as it does not isolate itself in a lie, it is blessed by the mercy and the love of Christ. Appearances are to be accepted for what they are. The accidents of a poor and transient existence have, nevertheless, an ineffable value. They can be transparent media in which we apprehend the presence of God in the world. It is possible to speak of the exterior self as a mask: to do so is not necessarily to reprove it. The mask that each man wears may well be a disguise not only for that man's inner self but for God, wandering as a pilgrim and exile in His own creation. (NS 295–96)

PART TWO

The World We Live In

Thomas Merton's view of the modern world evolved over time from a stark rejection of its empty promises to a deep compassion for its tragic limitations. In the passages that follow, Merton provides a social and spiritual framework for understanding life in the modern world.

UNQUIET CITY

We are living in the greatest revolution in history—a huge spontaneous upheaval of the entire human race: not the revolution planned and carried out by any particular party, race, or nation, but a deep elemental boiling over of all the inner contradictions that have ever been in man, a revelation of the chaotic forces inside everybody. This is not something we have chosen, nor is it something we are free to avoid.

This revolution is a profound spiritual crisis of the whole world, manifested largely in desperation, cynicism, violence, conflict, self-contradiction, ambivalence, fear and hope, doubt and belief, creation and destructiveness, progress and regression, obsessive attachments to images, idols, slogans, programs that only dull the general anguish for a moment until it bursts out everywhere in a still more acute and terrifying form. We do not know if we are building a fabulously wonderful world or destroying all that we have ever had, all that we have achieved!

All the inner force of man is boiling and bursting out, the good together with the evil, the good poisoned by evil and fighting it, the evil pretending to be good and revealing itself in the most dreadful crimes, justified and rationalized by the purest and most innocent intentions.   (CGB 54-55)

◆   ◆   ◆

I think the question of "turning to the world"* is in fact a question of being patient with the unprepossessing surface of it, in order to

*This phrase refers to the change in the Catholic Church, most notable during the reign of Pope John XXIII (1958-1963), away from isolation and toward an openness to the world. Pope

break through to the deep goodness that is underneath. But to my way of thinking, "the world" is precisely the dehumanized surface. What is under the surface, and often stifled and destroyed, is *more* than "the world": it is the spirit and likeness of God in men. Much of the ambiguity in talk about the world—especially mine—is that everyone tends to be quite selective about the elements he admits into his concept of "the world." My particular concept focuses on the sham, the unreality, the alienation, the forced systematization of life, and not on the human reality that is alienated and suppressed. This has to be made clear.   (CGB 234)

◆ ◆ ◆

The real trouble with "the world," in the bad sense which the Gospel condemns, is that it is a complete and systematic sham, and he who follows it ends not by living but by pretending he is alive, and justifying his pretense by an appeal to the general conspiracy of all the others to do the same.

It is this pretense that must be vomited out in the desert.* But when the monastery is only a way station to the desert, when it remains permanently that and nothing else, then one is neither in the world nor out of it. One lives marginally, with one foot in the general sham.   (CGB 310)

◆ ◆ ◆

We live in the time of no room, which is the time of the end. The time when everyone is obsessed with lack of time, lack of space,

---

John XXIII's final Papal Epistle was addressed to "all men of goodwill," not just to members of the Catholic Church.

*Merton admired Father Paul Evdokimov's essay on the Desert Fathers, particularly the line "One goes into the desert to vomit up the interior phantom, the doubter, the double" (CGB 309).

with saving time, conquering space, projecting into time and space the anguish produced within them by the technological furies of size, volume, quantity, speed, number, price, power and acceleration.

The primordial blessing, "increase and multiply," has suddenly become a hemorrhage of terror. We are numbered in billions, and massed together, marshalled, numbered, marched here and there, taxed, drilled, armed, worked to the point of insensibility, dazed by information, drugged by entertainment, surfeited with everything, nauseated with the human race and with ourselves, nauseated with life.

As the end approaches, there is no room for nature. The cities crowd it off the face of the earth. (RU 70)

◆ ◆ ◆

The city itself lives on its own myth. Instead of waking up and silently existing, the city people prefer a stubborn and fabricated dream; they do not care to be a part of the night, or to be merely of the world. They have constructed a world outside the world, against the world, a world of mechanical fictions which condemn nature and seek only to use it up, thus preventing it from renewing itself and man. (RU 10–11)

◆ ◆ ◆

All has become one, all has become indifferent, all has been leveled to equal meaninglessness. . . . It is not that all is "one" but all is "zero." Everything adds up to zero. Indeed, even the state, in the end, is zero. Freedom is then to live and die for zero. Is that what I want: to be beaten, imprisoned, or shot for zero? But to be shot for zero is not a matter of choice. It is not something one is required either to "want" or "not want." It is not even something one is able to foresee.

Zero swallows hundreds of thousands of victims every year, and the police take care of the details. Suddenly, mysteriously, without reason, your time comes, and while you are still desperately trying to make up your own mind what you imagine you might possibly be dying for, you are swallowed up by zero. Perhaps, subjectively, you have tried to convince *yourself* and have not wasted time convincing others. Nobody else is interested. What I have said so far concerns execution for a "political crime." But death in war is, in the same way, a kind of execution for nothing, a meaningless extinction, a swallowing up by zero. (CGB 92–93)

◆ ◆ ◆

We live in a society whose whole policy is to excite every nerve in the human body and keep it at the highest pitch of artificial tension, to strain every human desire to the limit and to create as many new desires and synthetic passions as possible, in order to cater to them with the products of our factories and printing presses and movie studios. (SSM 133)

◆ ◆ ◆

We live in a society that tries to keep us dazzled with euphoria in a bright cloud of lively and joy-loving slogans. Yet nothing is more empty and more dead, nothing is more insultingly insincere and destructive than the vapid grins on the billboards and the moron beatitudes in the magazines which assure us that we are all in bliss right now. I know of course that we are fools, but I do not think any of us are fools enough to believe that we are now in heaven, even though the Russians are breaking their necks in order to become as rich as we are. I think the constant realization that we are exhausting our vital spiritual energy in a waste of shame, the inescapable disgust at the idolatrous vulgarity of our commercial milieu (or the various other apocalyptic whoredoms that abound elsewhere on the face of the earth) is one of the main sources of our universal desperation.

(FAV 116)

◆ ◆ ◆

If we are fools enough to remain at the mercy of the people who want to sell us happiness, it will be impossible for us ever to be content with anything. How would they profit if we became content? We would no longer need their new product.

The last thing the salesman wants is for the buyer to become content. You are of no use in our affluent society unless you are always just about to grasp what you never have.

The Greeks were not as smart as we are. In their primitive way they put Tantalus* in hell. Madison Avenue, on the contrary, would convince us that Tantalus is in heaven. (CGB 84)

◆ ◆ ◆

Where men live huddled together without true communication, there seems to be greater sharing, and a more genuine communion. But this is not communion, only immersion in the general meaninglessness of countless slogans and clichés repeated over and over again so that in the end one listens without hearing and responds without thinking. The constant din of empty words and machine noises, the endless booming of loudspeakers end by making true

---

*Tantalus was a legendary Greek king of Lydia, who was punished for offenses against the gods by being made to stand in Hades within reach of food and drink that moved away whenever he tried to touch it.

communication and true communion almost impossible. Each individual in the mass is insulated by thick layers of insensibility. He doesn't care, he doesn't hear, he doesn't think. He does not act, he is pushed. He does not talk, he produces conventional sounds when stimulated by the appropriate noises. He does not think, he secretes clichés.   (NS 54–55)

◆ ◆ ◆

The poet who rebels completely against conventional Western society (Rimbaud, Baudelaire, the Beats) establishes that society more firmly in its complacent philistinism; he also strengthens its conviction that all artists are by necessity opium fiends and feeds its sense of magnanimity in tolerating such people.

What I mean to say by this is that the enemies of the artist's freedom are those who most profit by his *seeming* to be free, whether or not he is so.

And the artist himself, to the extent that he is dominated by introjected philistine condemnations of his art, pours out his energy and integrity in resisting these tyrannical pressures which come to him from within himself. His art then wastes itself in reaction against the anti-art of the society in which he lives (or he cultivates anti-art as a protest against the art cult of the society in which he lives).

(RU 166)

◆ ◆ ◆

The population of the affluent world is nourished on a steady diet of brutal mythology and hallucination, kept at a constant pitch of high tension by a life that is intrinsically violent in that it forces a large part of the population to submit to an existence which is humanly intolerable. . . . The problem of violence, then, is not the problem of a few rioters and rebels, but the problem of a whole structure which is outwardly ordered and respectable, and inwardly ridden by psychopathic obsessions and delusions.   (FAV 3)

◆ ◆ ◆

Never before has there been such a distance between the abject misery of the poor (still the great majority of mankind) and the absurd affluence of the rich. Our gestures at remedying this situation are well meant but almost totally ineffective. In many ways they only make matters worse (when for instance those who are supposed to be receiving aid realize that in fact most of it goes into the pockets of corrupt politicians who maintain the *status quo,* of which the misery of the poor is an essential part).

The problem of racism—by no means confined to the southern United States, South Africa, or Nazi Germany—is becoming a universal symptom of homicidal paranoia. The desperation of man who finds existence incomprehensible and intolerable, and who is only maddened by the insignificance of the means taken to alleviate his condition.

The fact that most men believe, as an article of faith, that we are now in a position to solve all our problems does not prove that this is so. On the contrary, this belief is so unfounded it is itself one of our greatest problems.   (CGB 60–61)

◆ ◆ ◆

The problems of the nations are the problems of mentally deranged people, but magnified a thousand times because they have the full, straight-faced approbation of a schizoid society, schizoid national structures, schizoid military and business complexes, and, need one add, schizoid religious sects.   (GON 3)

◆ ◆ ◆

I have learned that an age in which politicians talk about peace is an age in which everybody expects war: the great men of the earth would not talk of peace so much if they did not secretly believe it possible, with *one more war,* to annihilate their enemies forever. Always, "after just one more war" it will dawn, the new era of love: but first everybody who is hated must be eliminated. For hate, you see, is the mother of their kind of love.

Unfortunately the love that is to be born out of hate will never be born. Hatred is sterile; it breeds nothing but the image of its own empty fury, its own nothingness. Love cannot come of emptiness. It is full of reality. Hatred destroys the real being of man in fighting the fiction which it calls "the enemy." For man is concrete and alive, but "the enemy" is a subjective abstraction. A society that kills real men in order to deliver itself from the phantasm of a paranoid delusion is already possessed by the demon of destructiveness because it has made itself incapable of love. It refuses, *a priori,* to love. It is dedicated not to concrete relations of man with man, but only to abstractions about politics, economics, psychology, and even, sometimes, religion. (CP 374–75)

◆ ◆ ◆

Is this "the world"? Yes. It is the same wherever you have mass man. The basic pattern is identical in Russia, the United States, France. The materials and appearances differ, and in Western Europe perhaps the cut is a little more sophisticated. But it is the same suit of clothes, and same pair of ready-made pants, the same spiritual cretinism which in fact makes Christians and atheists indistinguishable.

All this is obviously irreversible. Whether one is "with" it or "against" it makes not the slightest difference. And perhaps that is why "believers" are tired of pretending that their "belief" somehow distinguishes them from others who are completely committed to these values. In fact, belief makes no earthly difference. For my own part, I am by my whole life committed to a certain protest and non-acquiescence, and that is why I am a monk. Yet I know that protest is not enough—is perhaps meaningless. Yet that is also why protest and non-acquiescence must extend to certain conceptions of monasticism which seem to me to be simply a fancy-dress adaptation of what we are claiming we have renounced.

As if, for instance, "leaving the world" were adequately summed up by those pictures of "the Trappist"* with his cowl over his head and his back to the camera, looking at a lake.   (cgb 36-37)

◆ ◆ ◆

This is no longer a time of systematic ethical speculation, for such speculation implies time to reason, and the power to bring social and individual action under the concerted control of reasoned principles upon which most men agree.

There is no time to reason out, calmly and objectively, the moral implications of technical developments which are perhaps already superseded by the time one knows enough to reason about them.

Action is not governed by moral reason but by political expediency and the demands of technology—translated into the simple abstract formulas of propaganda. These formulas have nothing to do with reasoned moral action, even though they may appeal to appar-

*The photo Merton is referring to here appeared on the inside flap of *The Sign of Jonas*, the sequel to *The Seven Storey Mountain*. The photo represented his publisher's attempt to "romanticize" the monastic life, and came to symbolize for Merton the conventional religious pieties found in some of his earlier works.

ent moral values—they simply condition the mass of men to react in a desired way to certain stimuli.

Men do not agree in moral reasoning. They concur in the emotional use of slogans and political formulas. There is no persuasion but that of power, of quantity, of pressure, of fear, of desire. Such is our present condition—and it is critical!

Bonhoeffer wrote, shortly before his death at the hands of the Nazis, that moral theorizing was outdated in such a time of crisis—a time of villains and saints, and of Shakespearian characters. "The villain and the saint have little to do with systematic ethical studies. They emerge from the primeval depths and by their appearance they tear open the infernal or the divine abyss from which they come and enable us to see for a moment into mysteries of which they had never dreamed."

And the peculiar evil of our time, Bonhoeffer continues, is to be sought not in the sins of the good, but in apparent virtues of the evil. A time of confirmed liars who tell the truth in the interest of what they themselves are—liars. A hive of murderers who love their children and are kind to their pets. A hive of cheats and gangsters who are loyal in pacts to do evil. Ours is a time of evil which is so evil that it can do good without prejudice to its own iniquity—it is no longer threatened by goodness. Such is Bonhoeffer's judgment of a world in which evil appears in the form of probity and righteousness. In such a time the moral theorist proves himself a perfect fool by taking the "light" at its face value and ignoring the abyss of evil underneath it. For him, as long as evil takes a form that is theoretically "permitted," it is good. He responds mentally to the abstract moral equation. His heart does not detect the ominous existential stink of moral death. (CGB 53–54)

❖   ❖   ❖

In our society, a society of business rooted in Puritanism, based on a pseudo-ethic of industriousness and thrift, to be rewarded by comfort, pleasure, and a good bank account, the myth of work is thought to justify an existence that is essentially meaningless and futile. There is, then, a great deal of busy-ness as people invent things to do when in fact there is very little to be done. Yet we are overwhelmed with jobs, duties, tasks, assignments, "missions" of every kind. At every moment we are sent north, south, east, and west by the angels of business and art, poetry and politics, science and war, to the four corners of the universe to decide something, to sign something, to buy and sell. We fly in all directions to sell ourselves, thus justifying the absolute nothingness of our lives. The more we seem to accomplish, the harder it becomes to really dissimulate our trifling, and the only thing that saves us is the common conspiracy not to advert to what is really going on.   (CGB 177)

◆   ◆   ◆

Businesses are, in reality, quasi-religious sects. When you go to work in one you embrace *a new faith.* And if they are really big businesses, you progress from faith to a kind of mystique. Belief in the product, preaching the product, in the end the product becomes the focus of a transcendental experience. Through "the product" one communes with the vast forces of life, nature, and history that are expressed in business. Why not face it? Advertising treats all products with the reverence and the seriousness due to sacraments.

Harrington says *(Life in the Crystal Palace):* "The new evangelism whether expressed in soft or hard selling, is a quasi-religious approach to business, wrapped in a hoax—a hoax voluntarily entered into by producers and consumers together. Its credo is that of belief-to-order. It is the truth-to-order as delivered by advertising

and public relations men, believed in by them and voluntarily believed by the public."*

Once again, it is the question of a game. Life is aimless, but one
invents a thousand aimless aims and then mobilizes a whole economy around them, finally declaring them to be transcendental, mystical, and absolute.

Compare our monastery and the General Electric plant in Louis-
ville. Which one is the more serious and more "religious" institu-
tion? One might be tempted to say "the monastery," out of sheer
habit. But, in fact, the religious seriousness of the monastery is like
sandlot baseball compared with the big-league seriousness of General Electric. It may in fact occur to many, including the monks, to
doubt the monastery and what it represents.

Who doubts G.E.?   (CGB 211)

◆   ◆   ◆

Popular religion has to a great extent betrayed man's inner spirit
and turned him over, like Samson, with his hair cut off and his
eyes dug out, to turn the mill of a self-frustrating and self-destroying
culture. The clichés of popular religion have in many cases become
every bit as hollow and as false as those of soap salesmen, and far
more dangerously deceptive because one cannot so easily verify the
claims made about the product. The sin of religiosity is that it has
turned God, peace, happiness, salvation and all that man desires
into products to be marketed in an especially attractive package deal.
In this, I think, the fault lies not with the sincerity of preachers and
religious writers, but with the worn-out presuppositions with which
they fare content to operate. The religious mind today is seldom

*Alan Harrington's book, published in 1959, was a minor masterpiece of social criticism,
exposing the psychological costs of what was then called "the rat race."

pertinently or prophetically critical. Oh, it is critical all right; but too often of wrong or irrelevant issues. There is still such a thing as straining at gnats and swallowing camels. But I wonder if we have not settled down too comfortably to accept passively the prevarications that the Gospels or the Prophets would have us reject with all the strength of our being. I am afraid the common combination of organizational jollity, moral legalism and nuclear crusading will not pass muster as a serious religion. It certainly has little to do with "spiritual life." (FAV 116–17)

◆ ◆ ◆

My thesis is now clear: in my opinion the root of our trouble is that our habits of thought and the drives that proceed from them are basically idolatrous and mythical. We are all the more inclined to idolatry because we imagine that we are of all generations the most enlightened, the most objective, the most scientific, the most progressive and the most humane. This, in fact, is an "image" of ourselves—an image which is false and is also the object of a cult. We worship ourselves in this image. The nature of our acts is determined in large measure by the demands of our worship. Because we have an image (simulacrum) of ourselves as fair, objective, practical and humane, we actually make it more difficult for ourselves to be what we think we are. Since our "objectivity" for instance is in fact an image of ourselves as "objective," we soon take our objectivity for granted, and instead of checking the facts, we simply manipulate the facts to fit our pious conviction. In other words, instead of taking care to examine the realities of our political or social problems, we simply bring out the idols in solemn procession. "We are the ones who are right, *they* are the ones who are wrong. We are the good guys, *they* are the bad guys. We are honest, *they* are crooks." In this confrontation of images, "objectivity" ceases to be a consistent attention to fact and becomes a devout and blind fidelity to myth. If the adversary is by definition wicked, then objectivity consists simply in refusing to believe that he can possibly be honest in any circumstances whatever. If facts seem to conflict with images, then we feel that we are being tempted by the devil, and we determine that we will be all the more blindly loyal to our images. To debate with the devil would be to yield! Thus in support of realism and objectivity we simply determine beforehand that we will be swayed by no fact whatever that does not accord perfectly with our own preconceived judgment. Objectivity becomes simple dogmatism.

(FAV 154–55)

◆ ◆ ◆

Is there any vestige of truth left in our declaration that we think for ourselves? Or do we even trouble to declare this any more? Perhaps the man who says he "thinks for himself" is simply one who does not think at all; because he has no fully articulate thoughts, he thinks he has his own incommunicable ideas. Or thinks that, if he once set his mind to it, he could have his own thoughts. But he just has not got around to doing this. I wonder if "democracies" are made up entirely of people who "think for themselves" in the sense of going around with blank minds which they imagine they *could* fill with their own thoughts if need be.

Well, the need has been desperately urgent, not for one year or ten, but for fifty, sixty, seventy, a hundred years. If, when thought is needed, nobody does any thinking, if everyone assumes that someone else is thinking, then it is clear that no one is thinking either for himself or for anybody else. Instead of thought, there is a vast, inhuman void full of words, formulas, slogans, declarations, echoes—ideologies! You can always reach out and help yourself to some of them. You don't even have to reach at all. Appropriate echoes already rise up in your mind—they are "yours." You realize of course that these are not yet "thoughts." Yet we "think" these formulas, with which the void in our hearts is provisionally entertained, can for the time being "take the place of thoughts"—while the computers make decisions for us.   (CGB 66)

◆　◆　◆

A few years ago a man who was compiling a book entitled *Success* wrote and asked me to contribute a statement on how I got to be a success. I replied indignantly that I was not able to consider myself a success in any terms that had a meaning to me. I swore I had spent my life strenuously avoiding success. If it so happened that I had once written a best seller, this was a pure accident, due to inattention and naiveté, and I would take very good care never to do the same again. If I had a message to my contemporaries, I said, it was surely this: Be anything you like, be madmen, drunks, and bastards of every shape and form, but at all costs avoid one thing: success. I heard no more from him, and I am not aware that my reply was published with the other testimonials.   (LL 10)

◆　◆　◆

The greatest need of our time is to clean out the enormous mass of mental and emotional rubbish that clutters our minds and makes all political and social life a mass illness. Without this house cleaning we cannot begin to *see*. Unless we *see*, we cannot think. The purification must begin with the mass media. How?   (CGB 64)

◆　◆　◆

In proportion as he becomes authentically aware of his own plight, man confronts the absurd—and finds it not in himself or in the objective world, but "in their presence together." Whereas he seeks to understand himself and his world by reason, he finds that the "only bond" between himself and the world is the absurd. He is caught by a desire for clarity that is frustrated by the irrational abuse of reason itself. If he consents to his situation, resigns himself to it, and convinces himself by his reasoning that things are just as they should be, he abdicates his dignity as a human person in order to enjoy the tranquility of a delusive "order." This delusion must be refused. The absurd must be faced. Anguish must not be evaded, for it is "the perpetual climate of the lucid man." Language must then be used not merely to rationalize and justify what is basically absurd, but to awaken in man the lucid anguish in which alone he is truly conscious of his condition and therefore able to revolt against the absurd. Then he will affirm, over against its "unreasonable silence," the human love and solidarity and devotion to life which give meaning to his own existence. "The doctrines that explain everything to me also debilitate me at the same time. They relieve me of the weight of my own life and yet I must carry it alone."*

(LE 275)

◆   ◆   ◆

The basic inner moral contradiction of our age is that, though we talk and dream about freedom (or say we dream of it, though I sometimes question that!), though we fight wars over it, our civilization is strictly *servile*. I do not use this term contemptuously, but in its original sense of "pragmatic," oriented exclusively to the useful, making use of means for material ends. The progress of technological culture has in fact been a progress in servility, that is in tech-

---

* All quoted phrases are from *The Myth of Sisyphus*, by Albert Camus (New York: Vintage Books, 1959).

niques of *using* material resources, mechanical inventions, etc., in order to get things done. This has, however, two grave disadvantages. First, the notion of the *gratuitous* and the *liberal* (the end in itself) has been lost. Hence we have made ourselves incapable of that happiness which transcends servility and simply rejoices in being for its own sake. Such "liberality" is in fact completely foreign to the technological mentality as we have it now (though not necessarily foreign to it in essence). Second, and inseparable from this, we have in practice developed a completely servile concept of man. Our professed ideals may still pay lip service to the dignity of the person, but without a sense of *being* and a respect for being, there can be no real appreciation of the person. We are so obsessed with *doing* that we have no time and no imagination left for *being*.

(CGB 281–82)

THE TECHNOLOGICAL IMPERATIVE

Science and technology are indeed admirable in many respects, and if they fulfill their promises, they can do much for man. But they can never solve his deepest problems. On the contrary, without wisdom, without the intuition and freedom that enable man to return to the root of his being, science can only precipitate him still further into the centrifugal flight that flings him, in all his compact and uncomprehending isolation, into the darkness of outer space without purpose and without objective. (FAV 224)

◆ ◆ ◆

Technology can elevate and improve man's life only on one condition: that it remains subservient to his *real* interests; that it respects his true being; that it remembers that the origin and goal of all being is in God. But when technology merely takes over all being for its own purposes, merely exploits and uses up all things in the pursuit of its own ends, and makes everything, including man himself, subservient to its processes, then it degrades man, despoils the world, ravages life, and leads to ruin. (CGB 230)

◆ ◆ ◆

It does us no good to make fantastic progress if we do not know how to live with it, if we cannot make good use of it, and if, in fact, our technology becomes nothing more than an expensive and complicated way of cultural disintegration. It is bad form to say such things, to recognize such possibilities. But they are possibilities, and they are not often intelligently taken into account. People get emotional about them from time to time, and then try to sweep them aside into forgetfulness. The fact remains that we have created for ourselves a culture which is not yet livable for mankind as a whole. (CGB 60)

◆ ◆ ◆

If technology really represented the rule of reason, there would be much less to regret about our present situation. Actually, technology represents the rule of quantity, not the rule of reason (quality = value = relation of means to authentic human ends). It is by means of technology that man the person, the subject of qualified and perfectible freedom, becomes *quantified,* that is, becomes part of a mass—mass man—whose only function is to enter anonymously into the process of production and consumption. He becomes on one side an implement, a "hand," or better, a "bio-physical link" between machines: on the other side he is a mouth, a digestive system and an anus, something *through which* pass the products of his technological world, leaving a transient and meaningless sense of enjoyment. The effect of a totally emancipated technology is the regression of man to a climate of moral infancy, in total dependence not on "mother nature" (such a dependence would be partly tolerable and human) but on the pseudo-nature of technology, which has replaced nature by a closed system of mechanisms with no purpose but that of keeping themselves going.

If technology remained in the service of what is higher than itself—reason, man, God—it might indeed fulfill some of the functions that are now mythically attributed to it. But becoming autonomous, existing only for itself, it imposes upon man its own irrational demands, and threatens to destroy him. Let us hope it is not too late for man to regain control. (CGB 64)

◆ ◆ ◆

The real root-sin of modern man is that, in ignoring and condemning *being,* and especially his own being, he has made his *existence* a disease and an affliction. And, strangely, be has done this with all kinds of vitalistic excuses, proclaiming at every turn that he stands on frontiers of new abundance and permanent bliss.

This ambiguity and arbitrariness appear most clearly in technology. There is nothing wrong with technology in itself. It could indeed serve to deepen and perfect the quality of men's existence and in some ways it *has* done this. As Lewis Mumford said: "Too many thought not only that mechanical progress would be a positive aid to human improvement, which is true, *but that mechanical progress is the equivalent of human improvement,* which turns out to be sheer nonsense."

We have not even begun to plumb the depths of nonsense into which this absurd error has plunged us. (CGB 201-202)

◆ ◆ ◆

It is precisely this illusion, that mechanical progress means human improvement, that alienates us from our own being and our own reality. It is precisely because we are convinced that our life, as such, is better if we have a better car, a better TV set, better toothpaste, etc., that we condemn and destroy our own reality and the reality of our natural resources. Technology was made for man, not man for technology. In losing touch with being and thus with God, we have fallen into a senseless idolatry of production and consumption for their own sakes. We have renounced the act of being and plunged ourselves into *process* for its own sake. We no longer know how to live, and because we cannot accept life in its reality life ceases to be a joy and becomes an affliction. And we even go so far as to blame God for it! The evil in the world is all of our own making, and it proceeds entirely from our ruthless, senseless, wasteful, destructive, and suicidal neglect of our own being. (CGB 202)

◆ ◆ ◆

The central problem of the modern world is the complete emancipation and autonomy of the technological mind at a time when unlimited possibilities lie open to it and all the resources seem to be at hand. Indeed, the mere fact of questioning this emancipation, this autonomy, is the number-one blasphemy, an unforgivable sin in the eyes of modern man, whose faith begins with this: science can do everything, science must be permitted do everything it likes, science is infallible and impeccable, all that is done by science is right. No matter how monstrous, no matter how *criminal* an act may be, if it is justified by science it is unassailable.

The consequence of this is that technology and science are now responsible to no power and submit to no control other than their own. Needless to say, the demands of ethics no longer have any meaning if they come in conflict with these autonomous powers. Technology has its own ethic of expediency and efficiency. What *can* be done efficiently *must* be done in the most efficient way—even if what is done happens, for example, to be genocide or the devastation of a country by total war. Even the long-term economic interests of society, or the basic needs of man himself, are not considered when they get in the way of technology. We waste our natural resources, as well as those of undeveloped countries, iron, oil, etc., in order to fill our cities and roads with a congestion of traffic that is in fact largely useless, and is a symptom of the meaningless and futile agitation of our own minds.   (CGB 62–63)

◆ ◆ ◆

We live in an age of bad dreams, in which the scientist and engineer possess the power to give external form to the phantasms of man's unconscious. The bright weapons that sing in the atmosphere, ready to pulverize the cities of the world, are the dreams of giants without a center. Their mathematical evolutions are hieratic rites devised by Shamans without belief. One is permitted to wish their dreams had been less sordid!

But perhaps they are also the emanations of our own subliminal self!   (CP 374)

◆ ◆ ◆

It is true that neither the ancient wisdoms nor the modern sciences are complete in themselves. They do not stand alone. They call for one another. Wisdom without science is unable to penetrate the full sapiential meaning* of the created and material cosmos. Science

*Theologians describe as *sapiential* the knowledge sought in the Bible's wisdom literature (Job, Psalms, Proverbs, Ecclesiastes, and the Song of Solomon), which concerns *who God is.*

without wisdom leaves man enslaved to a world of unrelated objects in which there is no way of discovering (or creating) order and deep significance in man's own pointless existence. The vocation of modern man was to bring about their union in preparation for a new age. The marriage was wrecked on the rocks of the white man's dualism and of the inertia, the incomprehension, of ancient and primitive societies. We enter the post-modern (perhaps the post-historic!) era in total disunity and confusion. But while the white man has always, naturally, blamed the traditional ancient cultures and the primitive "savage" whom he never understood, it is certainly clear that if the union of science and wisdom has so far not been successful it is not because the East would not listen to the West: the East has been all too willing to listen. The West has not been able to listen to the East, to Africa, and to the now practically extinct voice of primitive America. As a result of this the ancient wisdoms have themselves fallen into disrepute and Asia no longer dares listen to herself!   (GON 1–2)

◆   ◆   ◆

I believe the reason for the inner confusion of Western man is that our technological society has no longer any place in it for wisdom that seeks truth for its own sake, that seeks the fulness of being, that seeks to rest in an intuition of the very ground of all being. Without wisdom, the apparent opposition of action and contemplation, work and rest, of involvement and detachment, can never be resolved. Ancient and traditional societies, whether of Asia or of the West, always specifically recognized "the way" of the wise, the way of spiritual discipline in which there was at once wisdom and method,

---

This is in contrast to the more ethical wisdom sought in the Bible's prophetic literature, which concerns *what God wants us to do.*

and by which, whether in art, in philosophy, in religion, or in the monastic life, some men would attain to the inner meaning of being, they would experience this meaning for all their brothers, they would so to speak bring together in themselves the divisions or complications that confused the life of their fellows. By healing the divisions in themselves they would help heal the divisions of the whole world. They would realize in themselves that unity which is at the same time the highest action and the purest rest, true knowledge and selfless love, a knowledge beyond knowledge in emptiness and unknowing; a willing beyond will in apparent non-activity. They would attain to the highest striving in the absence of striving and of contention. (FAV 217–18)

EVENTS AND PSEUDO-EVENTS

Nine tenths of the news, as printed in the papers, is pseudo-news, manufactured events. Some days ten tenths. The ritual morning trance, in which one scans columns of newsprint, creates a peculiar form of generalized pseudo-attention to a pseudo-reality. This experience is taken seriously. It is one's daily immersion in "reality." One's orientation to the rest of the world. One's way of reassuring himself that he has not fallen behind. That he is still there. That he still counts!

My own experience has been that renunciation of this self-hypnosis, of this participation in the unquiet universal trance, is no sacrifice of reality at all. To "fall behind" in this sense is to get out of the big cloud of dust that everybody is kicking up, to breathe and to see a little more clearly. (FAV 151)

◆   ◆   ◆

The things that we do, the things that make our news, the things that are contemporary, are abominations of superstition, of idolatry, proceeding from minds that are full of myths, distortions, half-truths, prejudices, evasions, illusions, in a word—*simulacra*. Ideas and conceptions that look good but aren't. Ideals that claim to be humane and prove themselves, in their effects, to be callous, cruel, cynical, sometimes even criminal. (FAV 153)

◆ ◆ ◆

There are various ways of being happy, and every man has the capacity to make his life what it needs to be for him to have a reasonable amount of peace in it. Why then do we persecute ourselves with illusory demands, never content until we feel we have conformed to some standard of happiness that is not good for us only, but for *everyone*? Why can we not be content with the secret gift of the happiness that God offers us, without consulting the rest of the world? Why do we insist, rather, on a happiness that is approved by the magazines and TV? Perhaps because we do not believe in a happiness that is given to us for nothing. We do not think we can be happy with a happiness that has no price tag on it. (CGB 84)

◆ ◆ ◆

Clearly, the "powers" and "elements" which in Paul's day dominated men's minds through pagan religion or through religious legalism, today dominate us in the confusion and the ambiguity of the Babel of tongues that we call mass-society.* Certainly I do not con-

---

*The reference here is to Galatians 4: "When we were children we were slaves to the *elemental* forces of the universe. But when the time had fully come, God sent forth his Son"; and to Romans 13, where Paul advises Christians to submit to *the powers* of the civil authorities.

demn everything in the mass media. But how does one stop to separate the truth from the half-truth, the event from the pseudo-event,
reality from the manufactured image? It is in this confusion of images and myths, superstitions and ideologies that the "powers of the
air" govern our thinking—even our thinking about religion! Where
there is no critical perspective, no detached observation, no time to
ask the pertinent questions, how can one avoid being deluded and
confused?

Someone has to try to keep his head clear of static and preserve
the interior solitude and silence that are essential for independent
thought.

A monk loses his reason for existing if he simply submits to all
the routines that govern the thinking of everybody else. He loses his
reason for existing if he simply substitutes other routines of his own!
He is obliged by his vocation to have his own mind if not to speak
it. He has got to be a free man.

What did the radio say this evening? I don't know.   (FAV 150)

◆ ◆ ◆

The real violence exerted by propaganda is this: by means of apparent truth and apparent reason, it induces us to surrender our freedom and self-possession. It predetermines us to certain conclusions,
and does so in such a way that we imagine that we are fully free in
reaching them by our own judgment and our own thought. Propaganda *makes up our mind* for us, but in such a way that it leaves us
the sense of pride and satisfaction of men who have made up their
own minds. And, in the last analysis, propaganda achieves this effect
because we want it to. This is one of the few real pleasures left to
modern man: this illusion that he is thinking for himself when, in
fact, someone else is doing his thinking for him. And this someone
else is not a personal authority, the great mind of a genial thinker, it

is the mass mind, the general "they," the anonymous whole. One is left, therefore, not only with the sense that one has thought things out for himself, but that he has also reached the correct answer without difficulty—the answer which is shown to be correct because it is the answer of everybody. Since it is at once my answer and the answer of everybody, how should I resist it?   (CGB 216–17)

◆ ◆ ◆

I have watched TV twice in my life. I am frankly not terribly interested in TV anyway. Certainly I do not pretend that by simply refusing to keep up with the latest news I am therefore unaffected by what goes on, or free of it all. Certainly events happen and they affect me as they do other people. It is important for me to know about them too: but I refrain from trying to know them in their fresh condition as "news." When they reach me they have become slightly stale. I eat the same tragedies as others, but in the form of tasteless crusts. The news reaches me in the long run through books and magazines, and no longer as a stimulant. Living without news is like living without cigarettes (another peculiarity of the monastic life). The need for this habitual indulgence quickly disappears. So, when you hear news without the "need" to hear it, it treats you differently. And you treat it differently too.   (FAV 151)

◆ ◆ ◆

Today, with the enormous amplification of news and of opinion, we are suffering from more than acceptable distortions of perspective. Our supposed historical consciousness, over-informed and over-stimulated, is threatened with death by bloating, and we are overcome with a political elephantiasis which sometimes seems to make all actual forward motion useless if not impossible. But in addition to the sheer volume of information there is the even more portentous fact of falsification and misinformation by which those in power are often completely intent not only on misleading others but even on convincing themselves that their own lies are "historical truth."

(FAV 250)

◆ ◆ ◆

Our over-sensitive awareness of ourselves as responsible for "making history" is a grotesque illusion, and it leads us into the morass of pseudo-events. Those who are obsessed with "making history" are responsible for the banality of the bad news which comes more and more to constitute our "history." The Church that takes all this too literally and too seriously needs to go back and read the New Testament, not omitting the book of *Revelation*.

The genuine saving event, the encounter of man with Christ in his encounter of love and reconciliation with his fellowman, is generally *not newsworthy*. Not because there is an ingrained malice in journalists but because such events are not sufficiently visible. In trying to make them newsworthy, or visible, in trying to put them on TV, we often make them altogether incredible—or else reduce them to the common level of banality at which they can no longer be distinguished from pseudo-events.   (FAV 162–63)

◆ ◆ ◆

Reading the Vulgate I run across the Latin word *simulacrum* which has implications of a mask-like deceptiveness, of intellectual cheating, of an ideological shell-game. The word *simulacrum,* it seems to me, presents itself as a very suggestive one to describe an advertisement, or an over-inflated political presence, or that face on the TV screen. The word shimmers, grins, cajoles. It is a fine word for something monumentally phony. It occurs for instance in the last line of the First Epistle of John. But there it is usually translated as "idols," "Little Children, watch out for the simulacra!"—watch out for the national, the regional, the institutional images!

Does it not occur to us that if, in fact, we live in a society which is par excellence that of the *simulacrum,* we are the champion idolaters of all history? No, it does not occur to us, because for us an idol is nothing more than a harmless Greek statue, complete with a figleaf, in the corner of the museum. We have given up worrying about idols—as well as devils. And we are living in the age of science. How could we, the most emancipated of men, be guilty of superstition? Could science itself be our number one superstition?

You see where my rambling has brought me. To this: we are under judgment. And what for? For the primal sin. We are idolaters. We make *simulacra* and we hypnotize ourselves with our skill in creating these mental movies that do not appear to be idols because they are so alive! Because we are idolaters, because we have "exchanged the glory of the immortal God for the semblance of the likeness of mortal man, of birds, of quadrupeds, of reptiles . . ." we fulfill all the other requirements of those who are under God's wrath, as catalogued by Paul in Romans 1: 24–32.   (FAV 152–53)

◆ ◆ ◆

In primitive societies, where men are just beginning to read and [have] nothing to read but propaganda, we can say that they are its innocent victims. But in an evolved society there are no innocent victims of propaganda. Propaganda succeeds because men want it to succeed. It works on minds because those minds want to be worked on. Its conclusions bring apparent light and satisfaction because that is the kind of satisfaction that people are longing for. It leads them to actions for which they are already half prepared: all they ask is that these actions be justified. If war propaganda succeeds it is because people want war, and only need a few good reasons to justify their own desire.   (CGB 218)

◆ ◆ ◆

There is more than one way of morally liquidating the "stranger" and the "alien." It is sufficient to destroy, in some way, that in him which is different and disconcerting. By pressure, persuasion, or force one can impose on him one's own ideas and attitudes towards life. One can indoctrinate him, brainwash him. He is no longer different. He has been reduced to conformity with one's own outlook. Gog, who does nothing if not thoroughly, believes in the thorough liquidation of differences, and the reduction of everyone else to a carbon copy of himself. Magog is somewhat more quixotic: the stranger becomes part of his own screen of fantasies, part of the collective dream life which is manufactured for him on Madison Avenue and in Hollywood.* For all practical purposes, the stranger no longer exists. He is not even seen. He is replaced by a fantastic image. What is seen and approved, in a vague, superficial way, is the stereotype that has been created by the travel agency.

This accounts for the spurious cosmopolitanism of the naive tourist and traveling business man, who wanders everywhere with his camera, his exposure-meter, his spectacles, his sun glasses, his binoculars, and though gazing around him in all directions never sees what is there. He is not capable of doing so. . . . He does not know why he is traveling in the first place: indeed he is traveling at somebody else's suggestion. Even at home he is alien from himself. He is doubly alienated when he is out of his own atmosphere. He cannot possibly realize that the stranger has something very valuable, something irreplaceable to give him: something that can never be bought with money, never estimated by publicists, never exploited by political agitators: the spiritual understanding of a friend

---

*The reference here is to Revelation 20:7. In the final days, after the thousand-year reign of Christ, Gog and Magog will be gathered by Satan for a final battle on earth. Fire will come down from heaven and consume them. The Devil, who deceived them, will be thrown into the lake of fire. Merton is using these figures to reflect the potential apocalyptic clash between the Eastern and Western Blocs.

who belongs to a different culture. The tourist lacks nothing except brothers. For him these do not exist.

The tourist never meets anyone, never encounters anyone, never finds the brother in the stranger. This is his tragedy.   (CP 385–87)

◆ ◆ ◆

The great question then is how *do* we communicate with the modern world? If in fact communication has been reduced to pseudo-communication, to the celebration of pseudo-events and the irate clashing of incompatible myth-systems, how are we to avoid falling into this predicament? How are we to avoid the common obsession with pseudo-events in order to construct what seems to us to be a credible idol?

It is a nasty question, but it needs to be considered, for in it is contained the mystery of the evil of our time.

I do not have an answer to the question, but I suspect the root of it is this: if we love our own ideology and our own opinion instead of loving our brother, we will seek only to glorify our ideas and our institutions and by that fact we will make real communication impossible.

I think Bonhoeffer* was absolutely right when he said our real task is to bear in ourselves the fury of the world against Christ in order to reconcile the world with Christ.   (FAV 163)

*Dietrich Bonhoeffer (1906–1945)was a Protestant theologian who identified himself with the German Confessing Church, which opposed the pro-Nazi part of the Lutheran Church. During the war he became involved with anti-Hitler conspirators. He was arrested by the Nazis and hanged in Buchenwald concentration camp. His posthumous letters—along with his book, *The Cost of Discipleship*—explored the role of Christian ethics in a world "come of age."

PART THREE

Antidotes to Illusion

Merton believed that religious principles and practices that deepen our capacity for humility and compunction serve as allies to our "real selves" in their battle against the illusions of the modern world. Much of his best writing articulated the transformative power of these essential values.

TRUTH

A sincere man is not so much one who sees the truth and manifests it as he sees it, but one who loves the truth with pure love. But truth is more than an abstraction. It lives and is embodied in men and things that are real. And the secret of sincerity is, therefore, not to be sought in a philosophical love for abstract truth but in love for real people and real things—a love for God apprehended in the world around us. (NM 198)

◆ ◆ ◆

Here is a statement of Gandhi that sums up clearly and concisely the whole doctrine of nonviolence: "The way of peace is the way of truth." "Truthfulness is even more important than peacefulness. Indeed, *lying is the mother of violence.* A truthful man cannot long remain violent. He will perceive in the course of his research that he has no need to be violent, and he will further discover that so long as there is the slightest trace of violence in him, he will fail to find the truth he is searching." Why can we not believe this immediately? Why do we doubt it? Why does it seem impossible? Simply because we are all, to some extent, liars. (CGB 71)

◆ ◆ ◆

Basically our first duty today is to human truth in its existential reality, and this sooner or later brings us into confrontation with system and power which seek to overwhelm truth for the sake of particular interests, perhaps rationalized as ideals. Sooner or later this human duty presents itself in a form of crisis that cannot be evaded. At such a time it is very good, almost essential, to have at one's side others with a similar determination, and one can then be guided by a common inspiration and a communion in truth. Here true strength can be found. A completely isolated witness is much more difficult and dangerous. In the end that too may become necessary. But in any case we know that our only ultimate strength is in the Lord and in His Spirit, and faith must make us depend entirely on His will and providence. One must then truly be detached and free in order not to be held and impeded by anything secondary or irrelevant. Which is another way of saying that poverty also is our strength. (CFT 159)

◆ ◆ ◆

We are living under a tyranny of untruth which confirms itself in power and establishes a more and more total control over men in proportion as they convince themselves they are resisting error.

Our submission to plausible and useful lies involves us in greater and more obvious contradictions, and to hide these from ourselves we need greater and ever less plausible lies. The basic falsehood is the lie that we are totally dedicated to truth, and that we can remain dedicated to truth in a manner that is at the same time honest and exclusive: that we have the monopoly of all truth, just as our adversary of the moment has the monopoly of all error.

We then convince ourselves that we cannot preserve our purity of vision and our inner sincerity if we enter into dialogue with the enemy, for he will corrupt us with his error. We believe, finally, that truth cannot be preserved except by the destruction of the enemy— for, since we have identified him with error, to destroy him is to destroy error. The adversary,* of course, has exactly the same

*The "adversary" Merton is referring to, writing at the height of the Cold War, is the USSR.

thoughts about us and exactly the same basic policy by which he defends the "truth." He has identified us with dishonesty, insincerity, and untruth. He believes that, if we are destroyed, nothing will be left but truth. (CGB 56)

♦ ♦ ♦

Man's intelligence, however we may misuse it, is far too keen and too sure to rest for long in error. It may embrace a lie and cling to it stubbornly, believing it to be true: but it cannot find true rest in falsehood. The mind that is in love with error wears itself out with anxiety, lest its error be discovered for what it is. But the man who loves truth can already find rest in the acknowledgment of his mistakes, for that is the beginning of truth.

The first step toward finding God, Who is Truth, is to discover the truth about myself: and if I have been in error, this first step to truth is the discovery of my error. A false and illusory "experience" of what appears to be God's action in the soul may bring with it, for a moment, a kind of interior silence: the silence of a soul that rests in an illusion. But this silence is quickly disturbed by a deep undercurrent of unrest and noise. The tension of a soul trying to hold itself in silence, when it has no truth to appease it with a superior silence, is louder than the noise of big cities and more disturbing than the movement of an army. (NM 233)

♦ ♦ ♦

Sincerity must be bought at a price: the humility to recognize our innumerable errors, and fidelity in tirelessly setting them right.

The sincere man . . . is one who has the grace to know that he may be instinctively insincere, and that even his natural sincerity may become a camouflage for irresponsibility and moral cowardice: as if it were enough to recognize the truth, and do nothing about it!

(NM 192–93)

◆ ◆ ◆

Our task is not suddenly to burst out into the dazzle of utter unadulterated truth but laboriously to reshape an accurate and honest language that will permit communication between men on all social . . . levels, instead of multiplying a Babel of esoteric and technical tongues which isolate men in their specialties. (LE 272)

◆ ◆ ◆

Some things are too clear to be understood, and what you think is your understanding of them is only a kind of charm, a kind of incantation in your mind concerning that thing. This is not understanding: it is something you remember. So much for definition! We always have to go back and start from the beginning and make over all the definitions for ourselves again. (MA 53)

◆ ◆ ◆

Our thought should not merely be an answer to what someone else has just said. Or what someone else might have said. Our interior word must be more than an echo of the words of someone else. There is no point in being a moon to somebody else's sun, still less is there any justification for our being moons of one another, and hence darkness to one another, not one of us being a true sun.

It may seem that a child begins by *answering* his parents. This is not true. What is important in the child is his primal utterance, his response to *being*, his own free cries and signs, his admiration.

It is true that he has to learn language. Unfortunately in learning to speak, he also learns to answer *as expected*. Thus he learns more than language: he acquires, with words themselves, a kind of servitude. He gives out the words that are asked of him, that evoke a pleasant or approving response. He . . . engineers consent. He does not merely answer: he conforms, or he resists. He is already involved in public relations. (CGB 85)

◆　◆　◆

Truth, in things, is their reality. In our minds, it is the conformity of our knowledge with the things known. In our words, it is the conformity of our words to what we think. In our conduct, it is the conformity of our acts to what we are supposed to be. (NM 189)

◆　◆　◆

We make ourselves real by telling the truth. (NM 188)

SILENCE

There is in all visible things an invisible fecundity, a dimmed light, a meek namelessness, a hidden wholeness. This mysterious Unity and Integrity is Wisdom, the Mother of all, *Natura naturans*.* There is in all things an inexhaustible sweetness and purity, a silence that is a fount of action and joy. It rises up in wordless gentleness and flows out to me from the unseen roots of all created being,

*In classical Greek thought, "nature" had two aspects: the passive reality of our daily experience (*natura naturata,* or rested nature) and the active power that directs and governs life as well as the growth of a work of art (*natura naturans,* or creating nature).

welcoming me tenderly, saluting me with indescribable humility. This is at once my own being, my own nature, and the Gift of my Creator's Thought and Art within me, speaking as *Hagia Sophia,** speaking as my sister, Wisdom. (CP 363)

◆ ◆ ◆

Life is not to be regarded as an uninterrupted flow of words which is finally silenced by death. Its rhythm develops in silence, comes to the surface in moments of necessary expression, returns to deeper silence, culminates in a final declaration, then ascends quietly into the silence of Heaven which resounds with unending praise.

Those who do not know there is another life after this one, or who cannot bring themselves to live in time as if they were meant to spend their eternity in God, resist the fruitful silence of their own being by continual noise. Even when their own tongues are still, their minds chatter without end and without meaning, or they plunge themselves into the protective noise of machines, traffic, or radios. When their own noise is momentarily exhausted, they rest in the noise of other men.

How tragic it is that they who have nothing to express are continually expressing themselves, like nervous gunners, firing burst after burst of ammunition into the dark, where there is no enemy. The reason for their talk is: death. Death is the enemy who seems to confront them at every moment in the deep darkness and silence of their own being. So they keep shouting at death. They confound their lives with noise. They stun their own ears with meaningless words, never discovering that their hearts are rooted in a silence that is not death but life. They chatter themselves to death, fearing life as if it were death. (NM 261–62)

*Greek for "Holy Wisdom."

◆ ◆ ◆

Those who love their own noise are impatient of everything else. They constantly defile the silence of the forests and the mountains and the sea. They bore through silent nature in every direction with their machines, for fear that the calm world might accuse them of their own emptiness. The urgency of their swift movement seems to ignore the tranquillity of nature by pretending to have a purpose. The loud plane seems for a moment to deny the reality of the clouds and of the sky, by its direction, its noise, and its pretended strength. The silence of the sky remains when the plane has gone. The tranquillity of the clouds will remain when the plane has fallen apart. It is the silence of the world that is real. Our noise, our business, our purposes, and all our fatuous statements about our purposes, our business, and our noise: these are the illusion.   (NM 257)

◆ ◆ ◆

The deepest level of communication is not communication, but communion. It is wordless. It is beyond words, and it is beyond speech, and it is beyond concept. Not that we discover a new unity. We discover an older unity. My dear Brothers, we are already one. But we imagine that we are not. And what we have to recover is our original unity. What we have to be is what we are.   (AJ 308)

SOLITUDE

Ours is certainly a time for solitaries and hermits. But merely to reproduce the simplicity, austerity, and prayer of these primitive souls is not a complete or satisfactory answer. We must transcend them, and . . . liberate ourselves, in our own way, from involvement in a world that is plunging to disaster. But our world is different from theirs. Our involvement in it is more complete. Our danger is far more desperate.   (WOD 23)

◆ ◆ ◆

You will never find interior solitude unless you make some conscious effort to deliver yourself from the desires and the cares and the attachments of an existence in time and in the world.

Do everything you can to avoid the noise and the business of men. Keep as far away as you can from the places where they gather to cheat and insult one another, to exploit one another, to laugh at one another, or to mock one another with their false gestures of friendship. Be glad if you can keep beyond the reach of their radios. Do not bother with their unearthly songs. Do not read their advertisements.

The contemplative life certainly does not demand a self-righteous contempt for the habits and diversions of ordinary people. But nevertheless, no man who seeks liberation and light in solitude, no man who seeks spiritual freedom, can afford to yield passively to all the appeals of a society of salesmen, advertisers and consumers. There is no doubt that life cannot be lived on a human level without certain legitimate pleasures. But to say that all the pleasures which offer themselves to us as necessities are now "legitimate" is quite another story. A natural pleasure is one thing; an unnatural pleasure, forced upon the satiated mind by the importunity of a salesman, is quite another.   (NS 84–85)

◆ ◆ ◆

Keep your eyes clean and your ears quiet and your mind serene. Breathe God's air. Work, if you can, under His sky.

But if you have to live in a city and work among machines and ride in the subways and eat in a place where the radio makes you deaf with spurious news and where the food destroys your life and the sentiments of those around you poison your heart with boredom, do not be impatient, but accept it as the love of God and as a seed of solitude planted in your soul. If you are appalled by those things, you will keep your appetite for the healing silence of recollection. But meanwhile—keep your sense of compassion for the men who have forgotten the very concept of solitude. You, at least, know that it exists, and that it is the source of peace and joy. You can still hope for such joy. They do not even hope for it any more.

(NS 86–87)

◆   ◆   ◆

If a man does not know the value of his own loneliness, how can he respect another's solitude?

It is at once our loneliness and our dignity to have an incommunicable personality that is ours, ours alone and no one else's, and will be so forever.

When human society fulfills its true function the persons who form it grow more and more in their individual freedom and personal integrity. And the more each individual develops and discovers the secret resources of his own incommunicable personality, the more he can contribute to the life and the weal of the whole. Solitude is as necessary for society as silence is for language and air for the lungs and food for the body.

A community that seeks to invade or destroy the spiritual solitude of the individuals who compose it is condemning itself to death by spiritual asphyxiation. (NM 246–47)

◆   ◆   ◆

I ought to know, by now, that God uses everything that happens as a means to lead me into solitude. Every creature that enters my life, every instant of my days, will be designed to wound me with the realization of the world's insufficiency, until I become so detached that I will be able to find God alone in everything. Only then will all things bring me joy. (soj 51)

◆ ◆ ◆

Very few men are sanctified in isolation. Very few become perfect in absolute solitude.

Living with other people and learning to lose ourselves in the understanding of their weakness and deficiencies can help us to become true contemplatives. For there is no better means of getting rid of the rigidity and harshness and coarseness of our ingrained egoism, which is the one insuperable obstacle to the infused light and action of the Spirit of God.

Even the courageous acceptance of interior trials in utter solitude cannot altogether compensate for the work of purification accomplished in us by patience and humility in loving other men and sympathizing with their most unreasonable needs and demands.

There is always a danger that hermits will only dry up and solidify in their own eccentricity. Living out of touch with other people, they tend to lose that deep sense of spiritual realities, which only pure love can give. (ns 191)

◆ ◆ ◆

Today more than ever we need to recognize that the gift of solitude is not ordered for the acquisition of strange contemplative powers, but first of all to the recovery of one's deep self, and to the renewal of an authenticity which is twisted out of shape by the pretentious routines of a disordered togetherness. What the world asks of the priest today is that he should be first of all a *person* who can give himself because he has a self to give. And indeed, we cannot give Christ if we have not found him, and we cannot find him if we cannot find ourselves. (CIWA 267–68)

◆ ◆ ◆

Do you think the way to sanctity is to lock yourself up with your prayers and your books and the meditations that please and interest your mind, to protect yourself with many walls, against people you consider stupid? Do you think the way to contemplation is found in the refusal of activities and works which are necessary for the good of others but which happen to bore and distract you? Do you imagine that you will discover God by winding yourself up in a cocoon of spiritual and aesthetic pleasures, instead of renouncing all your tastes and desires and ambitions and satisfactions for the love of Christ, Who will not even live within you if you cannot find Him in other men? (NS 191–92)

◆ ◆ ◆

If you seek escape for its own sake and run away from the world only because it is (as it must be) intensely unpleasant, you will not find peace and you will not find solitude. If you seek solitude merely because it is what you prefer, you will never escape from the world and its selfishness; you will never have the interior freedom that will keep you really alone. (NS 87)

◆ ◆ ◆

You must be free, and not involved. Solitude is to be preserved not as a luxury but as a necessity: not for "perfection" so much as for simple "survival" in the life God has given you.

Hence, you must know when, how, and to whom you must say "no." This involves considerable difficulty at times. You must not hurt people, or want to hurt them, yet you must not placate them at the price of infidelity to higher and more essential .values.

People are constantly trying to use you to help them create the particular illusions by which they live. This is particularly true of the collective illusions which sometimes are accepted as ideologies. You must renounce and sacrifice the approval that is only a bribe enlisting your support of a collective illusion. You must not allow yourself to be represented as someone in whom a few of the favorite daydreams of the public have come true. You must be willing, if necessary, to become a disturbing and therefore an undesired person, one who is not wanted because he upsets the general dream. But be careful that you do not do this in the service of some other dream that is only a little less general and therefore seems to you the more real because it is more exclusive! (CGB 83)

◆ ◆ ◆

We tend to identify ourselves with those we love. We try to enter into their own souls and become what they are, thinking as they think, feeling as they feel, and experiencing what they experience.

But there is no true intimacy between souls who do not know how to respect one another's solitude. I cannot be united in love with a person whose very personality my love tends to obscure, to absorb, and to destroy. Nor can I awaken true love in a person who is invited, by my love, to be drowned in the act of drowning me with love. (NM 166)

◆ ◆ ◆

Secrecy and solitude are values that belong to the very essence of personality.

A person is a person insofar as he has a secret and is a solitude of his own that cannot be communicated to anyone else. If I love a person, I will love that which most makes him a person: the secrecy, the hiddenness, the solitude of his own individual being, which God alone can penetrate and understand.

A love that breaks into the spiritual privacy of another in order to lay open all his secrets and besiege his solitude with importunity does not love him: it seeks to destroy what is best in him, and what is most intimately his. (NM 244–45)

◆ ◆ ◆

This is what it means to seek God perfectly: to withdraw from illusion and pleasure, from worldly anxieties and desires, from the works that God does not want, from a glory that is only human display; to keep my mind free from confusion in order that my liberty may be always at the disposal of His will; to entertain silence in my heart and listen for the voice of God; to cultivate an intellectual freedom from the images of created things in order to receive the secret contact of God in obscure love; to love all men as myself; to rest in humility and to find peace in withdrawal from conflict and competition with other men; to turn aside from controversy and put away heavy loads of judgment and censorship and criticism and the whole burden of opinions that I have no obligation to carry; to have a will that is always ready to fold back within itself and draw all the powers of the soul down from its deepest center to rest in silent expectancy for the coming of God, poised in tranquil and effortless concentration upon the point of my dependence on Him; to gather all that I am, and have all that I can possibly suffer or do or be, and abandon them all to God in the resignation of a perfect love and blind faith and pure trust in God, to do His will.   (NS 45–46)

◆   ◆   ◆

The true solitary does not have to run away from others: they cease to notice him, because he does not share their love for an illusion. The soul that is truly solitary becomes perfectly colorless and ceases to excite either the love or the hatred of others by reason of its solitude. The true solitary can, no doubt, become a hated and a hunted person: but not by reason of anything that is in himself. He will only be hated if he has a divine work to do in the world. For his work will bring him into conflict with the world. His solitude, as such, creates no such conflict. Solitude brings persecution only when it takes the form of a "mission," and then there is something much more in it than solitude. For when the solitary finds that his solitude has taken on the character of a mission, he discovers that he has become a force that reacts on the very heart of the society in which he lives, a power that disturbs and impedes and accuses the forces of selfishness and pride, reminding others of their own need for solitude and for charity and for peace with God.   (NM 252–53)

◆   ◆   ◆

Solitude is so necessary both for society and for the individual that when society fails to provide sufficient solitude to develop the inner life of the persons who compose it, they rebel and seek false solitudes.   (NM 247)

◆   ◆   ◆

The world is the unquiet city of those who live for themselves and are therefore divided against one another in a struggle that cannot end, for it will go on eternally in hell. It is the city of those who are fighting for possession of limited things and for the monopoly of goods and pleasures that cannot be shared by all.

But if you try to escape from this world merely by leaving the city and hiding yourself in solitude, you will only take the city with you into solitude. . . .

For the flight from the world is nothing else but the flight from self-concern. And the man who locks himself up in private with his own selfishness has put himself into a position where the evil within him will either possess him like a devil or drive him out of his head.

That is why it is dangerous to go into solitude merely because you like to be alone.   (NS 78-79)

◆ ◆ ◆

We become solitaries not when we realize how alone we are, but when we sense something of the solitude of God. His solitude isolates us from everything around us, and yet makes us all the more truly the brothers of all things.

We cannot live for others until we have entered this solitude. If we try to live for them without first living entirely for God, we risk plunging with them all into the abyss.   (NM 228)

◆ ◆ ◆

How many there are who have solitude and do not love it, because their solitude is without recollection!* It is only loneliness. It does nothing to bring them to themselves. They are alone because in their solitude they are separated from God, and from other men, and even

*By *recollection* Merton' means a change of spiritual focus and an attuning of our soul to what is beyond ourselves, a turning of our being to spiritual things.

from themselves. They are like souls wandering out of hell and finding their way by mistake into Heaven, only to discover that Heaven
is more of a hell to them than hell itself. So it is with those who are
forced into the heaven of solitude and cannot taste its joy because
they know no recollection. (NM 228)

♦ ♦ ♦

The man who fears to be alone will never be anything but lonely,
no matter how much he may surround himself with people. But the
man who learns, in solitude and recollection, to be at peace with his
own loneliness, and to prefer its reality to the illusion of merely
natural companionship, comes to know the invisible companionship
of God. Such a one is alone with God in all places. (NM 228)

♦ ♦ ♦

My brother, perhaps in my solitude I have become as it were an
explorer for you, a searcher in realms which you are not able to
visit—except perhaps in the company of your psychiatrist. I have
been summoned to explore a desert area of man's heart in which
explanations no longer suffice, and in which one learns that only
experience counts. An arid, rocky, dark land of the soul, sometimes
illuminated by strange fires which men fear and peopled by specters
which men studiously avoid except in their nightmares. And in this
area I have learned that one cannot truly know hope unless he has
found out how like despair hope is. (MJ 171)

♦ ♦ ♦

In the refectory was read a short life of Saint Benedict Joseph Labre*
who is definitely one of my favorites. The only way he could find

*Patron saint of the lost and homeless (1748–1783) .

solitude was by being the most despised person in a crowd—going so low that everybody ignored him, although he had to work to keep himself there: refusing friendship, practically never speaking, regarding everyone who treated him kindly as a benefactor, not as a friend.

There is something in my nature that makes me dream of being a tramp but from what I know of my experiences at being one, sanctity does not lie that way for me. I was always strictly a tourist even when I traveled on foot or hitched rides. And a respectable one too, in the pejorative sense of the word respectable. Even as a Trappist I am woefully respectable, though not conventional. I have no fleas, either, because I don't like fleas and I suppose I'm not the kind that becomes sanctified by lice—although one never can tell what the future holds in store. (SOJ 153–54)

PRAYER, MEDITATION, CONTEMPLATION

If we really want prayer, we'll have to give it time. We must slow down to a human tempo and we'll begin to have time to listen. And as soon as we listen to what's going on, things will begin to take shape by themselves.

This is what the Zen people do. They give a great deal of time to doing whatever they need to do. That's what we have to learn when it comes to prayer. We have to give it time.

What truly matters is not how to get the most out of life, but how to recollect yourself so that you can fully give yourself.

What is keeping us back from living lives of prayer? Perhaps we don't really want to pray. This is the thing we have to face. Before this we took it for granted that we were totally dedicated to this desire for prayer. Somebody else was stopping us.

It is a risky thing to pray, and the danger is that our very prayers get between God and us. The great thing in prayer is not to pray, but to go directly to God. If saying your prayers is an obstacle to prayer, cut it out. Let Jesus pray. Thank God Jesus is praying. Forget yourself. Enter into the prayer of Jesus. Let him pray in you.

The best way to pray is: stop. Let prayer pray within you, whether you know it or not. This means a deep awareness of your true inner identity. . . .

There are no levels. Any moment you can break through into the underlying unity which is God's gift in Christ. In this end, Praise praises. Thanksgiving gives thanks. Jesus prays. Openness is all.

(CNP 56–57)

◆　◆　◆

All prayer, reading, meditation and all the activities of the monastic life are aimed at *purity of heart,* an unconditional and totally humble surrender to God, a total acceptance of ourselves and of our situation as willed by Him. It means the renunciation of all deluded images of ourselves, all exaggerated estimates of our own capacities, in order to obey God's will as it comes to us in the difficult demands of life in its exacting truth. *Purity of heart* is then correlative to a new spiritual identity—the "self" as recognized in the context of realities willed by God. Purity of heart is the enlightened awareness of the new man, as opposed to the complex and perhaps rather disreputable fantasies of the "old man."

Meditation is then ordered to this new insight, this direct knowledge of the self in its higher aspect. (CTP 68)

◆　◆　◆

We are going to have to create a new language of prayer. And this new language of prayer has to come out of something which transcends all our traditions, and comes out of the immediacy of love.

(AJ 318)

◆　◆　◆

The great thing is prayer. Prayer itself. If you want a life of prayer, the way to get it is by praying. We were indoctrinated so much into means and ends that we don't realize that there is a different dimension in the life of prayer. In technology you have this horizontal progress, where you must start at one point and move to another and then another. But that is not the way to build a life of prayer. In prayer we discover what we already have. You start where you are and you deepen what you already have. And you realize that you are already there. (CNP 56)

◆　◆　◆

If you have never had any distractions you don't know how to pray. For the secret of prayer is a hunger for God and for the vision of God, a hunger that lies far deeper than the level of language or affection. And a man whose memory and imagination are persecuting him with a crowd of useless or even evil thoughts and images may sometimes be forced to pray far better, in the depths of his murdered heart, than one whose mind is swimming with clear concepts and brilliant purposes and easy acts of love.

That is why it is useless to get upset when you cannot shake off distractions. In the first place, you must realize that they are often unavoidable in the life of prayer. The necessity of kneeling and suffering submersion under a tidal wave of wild and inane images is one of the standard trials of the contemplative life. If you think you are obliged to stave these things off by using a book and clutching at its sentences the way a drowning man clutches at straws, you have the privilege of doing so, but if you allow your prayer to degenerate into a period of simple spiritual reading you are losing a great deal of fruit. You would profit much more by patiently resisting distractions and learning something of your own helplessness and incapacity. And if your book merely becomes an anesthetic, far from helping your meditation it has probably ruined it. (NS 221–22)

◆　◆　◆

Prayer and meditation have an important part to play in opening up new ways and new horizons. If our prayer is the expression of a deep and grace-inspired desire for newness of life—and not the mere blind attachment to what has always been familiar and "safe"—God will act in us and through us to renew the Church by preparing, in prayer, what we cannot yet imagine or understand. In this way our prayer and faith today will be oriented toward the future which we ourselves may never see fully realized on earth. (CIWA 164–65)

◆　◆　◆

The monk who is truly a man of prayer and who seriously faces the challenge of his vocation in all its depth is by that very fact exposed to existential dread. He experiences in himself the emptiness, the lack of authenticity, the quest for fidelity, the "lostness" of modern man, but he experiences all this in an altogether different and deeper way than does man in the modern world, to whom this disconcerting awareness of himself and of his world comes rather as an experience of boredom and of spiritual disorientation. The monk confronts his own humanity and that of his world at the deepest and most central point where the void seems to open out into black despair. The monk confronts this serious possibility, and rejects it, as Camusian man confronts "the absurd" and transcends it by his freedom. The option of absolute despair is turned into perfect hope by the pure and humble supplication of monastic prayer. The monk faces the worst, and discovers in it the hope of the best. From the darkness comes light. From death, life. From the abyss there comes, unaccountably, the mysterious gift of the Spirit sent by God to make all things new, to transform the created and redeemed world, and to re-establish all things in Christ.

This is the creative and healing work of the monk.   (CTP 25)

◆ ◆ ◆

The purest prayer is something on which it is impossible to reflect until after it is over. And when the grace has gone we no longer seek to reflect on it, because we realize that it belongs to another order of things, and that it will be in some sense debased by our reflecting on it. Such prayer desires no witness, even the witness of our own souls. It seeks to keep itself entirely hidden in God. The experience remains in our spirit like a wound, like a scar that will not heal. But we do not reflect upon it. This living wound may become a source of knowledge, if we are to instruct others in the ways of prayer; or else it may become a bar and an obstacle to knowledge, a seal of silence set upon the soul, closing the way to words and thoughts, so that we can say nothing of it to other men.   (NM 50–51)

◆ ◆ ◆

Meditation is almost all contained in this one idea: the idea of *awakening* our interior self and attuning ourselves inwardly to the Holy Spirit, so that we will be able to respond to His grace. In mental prayer, over the years, we must allow our interior perceptivity to be refined and purified. We must attune ourselves to unexpected movements of grace, which do not fit our own preconceived ideas of the spiritual life at all, and which in no way flatter our own ambitious aspirations.

We must be ready to cooperate not only with graces that console, but with graces that humiliate us. Not only with lights that exalt us, but with lights that blast our self-complacency. Much of our coldness and dryness in prayer may well be a kind of unconscious defense against grace. Without realizing it, we allow our nature to desensitize our souls so that we cannot perceive graces which we intuitively foresee may prove to be painful.

Meditation is then always to be associated in practice with abandonment to the will and action of God. It goes hand in hand with self-renunciation and with obedience to the Holy Spirit. Meditation that does not seek to bring our whole being into conformity with God's will must naturally remain sterile and abstract. But any sincere interior prayer that really seeks this one all important end—our conformity to God's will in our regard—cannot fail to be rewarded by grace. It will prove, without question, to be one of the most sanctifying forces in our lives. And St. Teresa of Avila believed that no one who was faithful to the practice of meditation could possibly lose his soul. (SD&M 85-86)

◆   ◆   ◆

We must approach our meditation realizing that "grace," "mercy" and "faith" are not permanent inalienable possessions which we gain by our efforts and retain as though by right, provided that we behave ourselves. They are *constantly renewed gifts.* The life of grace in our hearts is renewed from moment to moment, directly and personally by God in His love for us. Hence the "grace of meditation" (in the sense of "prayer of the heart") is also a special gift. It should never be taken for granted. Though we can say it is a "habit" which is in some sense permanently present to us, when we have received it, yet it is never something which we can claim as though by right and use in a completely autonomous and self-determining manner according to our own good pleasure, without regard for God's will— though we can make an autonomous use of our *natural* gifts. The gift of prayer is inseparable from another grace: that of humility, which makes us realize that the very depths of our being and life are meaningful and real only in so far as they are oriented toward God as their source and their end. (CTP 69–70)

◆　◆　◆

Meditation is a twofold discipline that has a twofold function.

First it is supposed to give you sufficient control over your mind and memory and will to enable you to recollect yourself and withdraw from exterior things . . . and second—this is the real end of meditation—it teaches you how to become aware of the presence of God; and most of all it aims at bringing you to a state of almost constant loving attention to God, and dependence on Him.

(NS 217)

◆　◆　◆

A current of useless interior activity constantly surrounds and defends an illusion.

I cannot find God unless I renounce this useless activity, and I cannot renounce this activity unless I let go of the illusion it defends. And I cannot get rid of an illusion unless I recognize it for an illusion. (NM 232)

◆　◆　◆

What we need is not a false peace which enables us to evade the implacable light of judgment, but the grace courageously to accept the bitter truth that is revealed to us; to abandon our inertia, our egoism and submit entirely to the demands of the Spirit, praying earnestly for help, and giving ourselves generously to *every effort asked of us by God.*

A method of meditation or a form of contemplation that merely produces the illusion of having "arrived somewhere," of having achieved security and preserved one's familiar status by playing a part, will eventually have to be unlearned in dread—or else we will be confirmed in the arrogance, the impenetrable self-assurance of the Pharisee. He will become impervious to the deepest truths. We will be closed to all who do not participate in our illusion. We will live "good lives" that are basically inauthentic, "good" only as long as they permit us to remain established in our respectable and impermeable identities. The "goodness" of our lives depends on the security afforded by relative wealth, recreation, spiritual comfort, and a solid reputation for piety. Such "goodness" is preserved by routine and the habitual avoidance of serious risk—indeed of serious challenge. (CTP 103–104)

◆ ◆ ◆

By meditation I penetrate the inmost ground of my life, seek the full understanding of God's will for me, of God's mercy to me, of my absolute dependence upon him. But this penetration must be authentic. It must be something genuinely *lived* by me. This in turn depends on the authenticity of my whole concept of my life, and of my purposes. But my life and aims tend to be artificial, inauthentic, as long as I am simply trying to adjust my actions to certain exterior norms of conduct that will enable me to play an approved part in the society in which I live. After all, this amounts to little more than learning a *role.* Sometimes methods and programs of meditation are aimed simply at this: learning to play a religious role. The idea of the "imitation" of Christ and of the saints can degenerate into mere *impersonation,* if it remains only exterior. (CTP 68–69)

◆ ◆ ◆

When we seem to possess and use our being and natural faculties in a completely autonomous manner, as if our individual ego were the pure source and end of our own acts, then we are in illusion and our acts, however spontaneous they may seem to be, lack spiritual meaning and authenticity.

Consequently: first of all our meditation should begin with the realization of our nothingness and helplessness in the presence of God. This need not be a mournful or discouraging experience. On the contrary, it can be deeply tranquil and joyful since it brings us in direct contact with the source of all joy and all life. But one reason why our meditation never gets started is perhaps that we never make this real, serious return to the center of our own nothingness before God. Hence we never enter into the deepest reality of our relationship with him.

In other words we meditate merely "in the mind," in the imagination, or at best in the desires, considering religious truths from a detached objective viewpoint. We do not begin by seeking to "find our heart," that is to sink into a deep awareness of the ground of our identity before God and in God. "Finding our heart" and recovering this awareness of our inmost identity implies the recognition that our external, everyday self is to a great extent a mask and a fabrication. It is not our true self. And indeed our true self is not easy to find. It is hidden in obscurity and "nothingness," at the center where we are in direct dependence on God. But since the reality of all Christian meditation depends on this recognition, our attempt to meditate without it is in fact self-contradictory. It is like trying to walk without feet. (CTP 70–71)

◆ ◆ ◆

Even the capacity to recognize our condition before God is itself a grace. We cannot always attain it at will. To learn meditation does not mean learning an artificial technique for infallibly producing "compunction" and the "sense of our nothingness" whenever we please. On the contrary, this would be the result of violence and would be inauthentic. Meditation implies the capacity to *receive* this grace whenever God wishes to grant it to us, and therefore a permanent disposition to humility, attention to reality, receptivity, pliability. To learn to meditate then means to gradually get free from habitual hardness of heart, torpor and grossness of mind, due to arrogance and non-acceptance of simple reality, or resistance to the concrete demands of God's will.

If in fact our hearts remain apparently indifferent and cold, and we find it morally impossible to "begin" meditating in this way, then we should at least realize that this coldness is itself a sign of our need and of our helplessness. We should take it accordingly as a motive for prayer. We might also reflect that perhaps without meaning to we have fallen into a spirit of routine, and are not able to see how to recover our spontaneity without God's grace, for which we must wait patiently, but with earnest desire. This waiting itself will be for us a school of humility.   (CTP 71)

◆ ◆ ◆

The worst thing that can happen to a person who is already divided up into a dozen different compartments is to seal off yet another compartment and tell him that this one is more important than all the others, and that he must henceforth exercise a special care in keeping it separate from them. That is what tends to happen when contemplation is unwisely thrust without warning upon the bewilderment and distraction of Western man. The Eastern traditions have the advantage of disposing the person more naturally for contemplation.

The first thing that you have to do, before you start thinking about such a thing as contemplation, is to try to recover your basic natural unity, to reintegrate your compartmentalized being into a coordinated and simple whole, and learn to live as a unified human person. This means that you have to bring back together the fragments of your distracted existence so that when you say "I" there is really someone present to support the pronoun you have uttered.

(CQR 3)

◆ ◆ ◆

The most usual entrance to contemplation is through a desert of aridity in which, although you see nothing and feel nothing and apprehend nothing and are conscious only of a certain interior suffering and anxiety, yet you are drawn and held in this darkness and dryness because it is the only place in which you can find any kind of stability and peace. As you progress, you learn to rest in this arid quietude, and the assurance of a comforting and mighty presence at the heart of this experience grows on you more and more, until you gradually realize that it is God revealing Himself to you in a light that is painful to your nature and to all its faculties, because it is infinitely above them and because its purity is at war with your own selfishness and darkness and imperfection. (NM 275–76)

◆ ◆ ◆

Contemplative prayer is, in a way, simply the preference for the desert, for emptiness, for poverty. One has begun to know the meaning of contemplation when he intuitively and spontaneously seeks the dark and unknown path of aridity in preference to every other way. The contemplative is one who would rather not know than know. Rather not enjoy than enjoy. Rather not have *proof* that God loves him. He accepts the love of God on faith, in defiance of all apparent evidence. This is the necessary condition, and a very paradoxical condition, for the mystical experience of the reality of God's presence and of his love for us. Only when we are able to "let go" of everything within us, all desire to see, to know, to taste and to experience the presence of God, do we truly become able to experience that presence with the overwhelming conviction and reality that revolutionize our entire inner life.   (CTP 89)

◆ ◆ ◆

The contemplative life isn't something objective that is "there" and to which, after fumbling around, you finally gain access. The contemplative life is a dimension of our subjective existence. Discovering the contemplative life is a new self-discovery. One might say it is the flowering of a deeper identity on an entirely different plane from a mere psychological discovery, a paradoxical new identity that is found only in loss of self. To find one's self by losing one's self: that is part of "contemplation." Remember the Gospel, "He who would save his life must lose it"?*   (CIWA 340)

◆ ◆ ◆

Contemplation is the highest expression of man's intellectual and spiritual life. It is that life itself, fully awake, fully active, fully aware that it is alive. It is spiritual wonder. It is spontaneous awe at the sacredness of life, of being. It is gratitude for life, for awareness and

*Matthew 16:25.

for being. It is a vivid realization of the fact that life and being in us proceed from an invisible, transcendent . . . Source. . . . It is, above all, awareness of the reality of that Source. It *knows* the Source, obscurely, inexplicably, but with a certitude that goes both beyond reason and beyond simple faith. (NS 1)

◆ ◆ ◆

Contemplation is not and cannot be a function of this external self. There is an irreducible opposition between the deep transcendent self that awakens only in contemplation, and the superficial, external self which we commonly identify with the first person singular. We must remember that this superficial "I" is not our real self. It is our "individuality" and our "empirical self" but it is not truly the hidden and mysterious person in whom we subsist before the eyes of God. The "I" that works in the world, thinks about itself, observes its own reactions and talks about itself is not the true "I" that has been united to God in Christ. It is at best the vesture, the mask, the disguise of that mysterious and unknown "self" whom most of us never discover until we are dead.* Our external, superficial self is not eternal, not spiritual. Far from it. This self is doomed to disappear as completely as smoke from a chimney. It is utterly frail and evanescent. Contemplation is precisely the awareness that this "I" is really "not I" and the awakening of the unknown "I" that is beyond observation and reflection and is incapable of commenting upon itself. (NS 7)

◆ ◆ ◆

*"Hell" can be described a a perpetual alienation from our true being, our true self, which is in God. [Merton's original footnote.]

The contemplative way is in no sense a deliberate "technique" of self-emptying in order to produce an esoteric experience. It is the paradoxical response to an almost incomprehensible call from God, drawing us into solitude, plunging us into darkness and silence, not to withdraw and protect us from peril, but to bring us safely through untold dangers by a miracle of love and power.

The contemplative way is, in fact, not a way. Christ alone is the way, and he is invisible. The "desert" of contemplation is simply a metaphor to explain the state of emptiness which we experience when we have left all ways, forgotten ourselves and taken the invisible Christ as our way. (CTP 92)

❖ ❖ ❖

One of the first things to learn if you want to be a contemplative is how to mind your own business.

Nothing is more suspicious, in a man who seems holy, than an impatient desire to reform other men.

A serious obstacle to recollection is the mania for directing those you have not been appointed to direct, reforming those you have not been asked to reform, correcting those over whom you have no jurisdiction. How can you do these things and keep your mind at rest? Renounce this futile concern with other men's affairs!

Pay as little attention as you can to the faults of other people. And none at all to their natural defects and eccentricities. (NS 255)

❖ ❖ ❖

The contemplative life must provide an area, a space of liberty, of silence, in which possibilities are allowed to surface and new choices—beyond routine choice—become manifest. It should create a new experience of time, not as stopgap, stillness, but as "temps

vierge"*—not a blank to be filled or an untouched space to be con-
quered and violated, but a space which can enjoy its own potentiali-
ties and hopes—and its own presence to itself. One's *own* time. But
not dominated by one's own ego and its demands. Hence open to
others—*compassionate* time, rooted in the sense of common illusion
and in criticism of it. (AJ 117)

◆ ◆ ◆

The most dangerous man in the world is the contemplative who is
guided by nobody. He trusts his own visions. He obeys the attrac-
tions of an interior voice but will not listen to other men. He identifies the will of God with anything that makes him feel, within his
own heart, a big, warm, sweet interior glow. The sweeter and the
warmer the feeling is the more he is convinced of his own infallibil-
ity. And if the sheer force of his own self-confidence communicates
itself to other people and gives them the impression that he is really
a saint, such a man can wreck a whole city or a religious order or
even a nation. The world is covered with scars that have been left
in its flesh by visionaries like these.

However, very often these people are nothing more than harmless
bores. They have wandered into a spiritual blind-alley and there
they rest in a snug little nest of private emotions. No one else can
really bring himself either to envy or admire them, because even
those who know nothing of the spiritual life can somehow sense that
these are men who have cheated themselves out of reality and have
come to be content with a fake.

They seem to be happy, but there is nothing inspiring or conta-

*The French term *temps vierge* literally means "virginal time" and by extension, "first flowering."

gious about their happiness. They seem to be at peace, but their peace is hollow and restless. They have much to say, and everything they say is a message with a capital "M," and yet it convinces nobody. Because they have preferred pleasure and emotion to the austere sacrifices imposed by genuine faith, their souls have become stagnant. The flame of true contemplation has gone out.

When you are led by God into the darkness where contemplation is found, you are not able to rest in the false sweetness of your own will. The fake interior satisfaction of self-complacency and absolute confidence in your own judgment will never be able to deceive you entirely: it will make you slightly sick and you will be forced by a vague sense of interior nausea to gash yourself open and let the poison out. (NS 194–96)

◆ ◆ ◆

When the next step comes, you do not take the step, you do not know the transition, you do not fall into anything. You do not go anywhere, and so you do not know the way by which you got there or the way by which you come back afterward. You are certainly not lost. You do not fly. There is no space, or there is all space: it makes no difference.

The next step is not a step.

You are not transported from one degree to another.

What happens is that the separate entity that is *you* apparently disappears and nothing seems to be left but a pure freedom indistinguishable from infinite Freedom, love identified with Love. Not two loves, one waiting for the other, striving for the other, seeking for the other, but Love Loving in Freedom.

Would you call this experience? I think you might say that this only becomes an experience in a man's memory. Otherwise it seems wrong even to speak of it as something that happens. Because things that happen have to happen to some subject, and experiences have to be experienced by someone. But here the subject of any divided or limited or creature experience seems to have vanished. You are not you, you are fruition. If you like, you do not have an experience, you become Experience: but that is entirely different, because you no longer exist in such a way that you can reflect on yourself or see yourself having an experience, or judge what is going on, if it can be said that something is going on that is not eternal and unchanging and an activity so tremendous that it is infinitely still.

And here all adjectives fall to pieces. Words become stupid. Everything you say is misleading—unless you list every possible experience and say: *"That is not what it is." "That is not what I am talking about."*

Metaphor has now become hopeless altogether. Talk about "darkness" if you must: but the thought of darkness is already too dense and too coarse. Anyway, it is no longer darkness. You can speak of "emptiness" but that makes you think of floating around in space: and this is nothing spatial. (NS 282–84)

◆ ◆ ◆

The way to contemplation is an obscurity so obscure that it is no longer even dramatic. There is nothing in it that can be grasped and cherished as heroic or even unusual. And so, for a contemplative, there is supreme value in the ordinary everyday routine of work, poverty, hardship and monotony that characterize the lives of all the poor, uninteresting and forgotten people in the world. . . .

The surest asceticism is the bitter insecurity and labor and nonentity of the really poor. To be utterly dependent on other people. To be ignored and despised and forgotten. To know little of respectability or comfort. To take orders and work hard for little or no money:

it is a hard school, and one which most pious people do their best
to avoid. (NS 250)

◆ ◆ ◆

No one teaches contemplation except God, Who gives it. The best
you can do is write something or say something that will serve as an
occasion for someone else to realize what God wants of him.

(NS 250)

◆ ◆ ◆

The contemplative life has nothing to tell you except to reassure you
and say that if you dare to penetrate your own silence and dare to
advance without fear into the solitude of your own heart, and risk
the sharing of that solitude with the lonely other who seeks God
through you and with you, then you will truly recover the light
and the capacity to understand what is beyond words and beyond
explanations because it is too close to be explained: it is the intimate
union in the depths of your own heart, of God's spirit and your own
secret inmost self, so that you and He are in truth One Spirit.

(MJ 173)

MONASTICISM

Man has an instinctive need for harmony and peace, for tranquility,
order and meaning. None of those seem to be the most salient char-
acteristics of modern society. A book written in a monastery where
the traditions and rites of a more contemplative age are still alive
and still practiced, could not help but remind men that there had

once existed a more leisurely and more spiritual way of life—and that this was the way of their ancestors. Thus even into the confused pattern of Western life is woven a certain memory of contemplation. It is a memory so vague and so remote that it is hardly understood, and yet it can awaken the hope of recovering inner peace. In this hope, modern man can perhaps entertain, for a brief time, the dream of a contemplative life and of a higher spiritual state of quiet, of rest, of untroubled joy. But a sense of self-deception and guilt immediately awakens a reaction of despair, disgust, a rejection of the dream and a commitment to total activism. We must face the fact that the mere thought of contemplation is one which deeply troubles the person who takes it seriously. It is so contrary to the modern way of life, so apparently alien, so seemingly impossible, that the modern man who even considers it finds, at first, that his whole being rebels against it.   (HR 85)

◆ ◆ ◆

The monastic life is in a certain sense scandalous. The monk is precisely a *man who has no specific task*. He is liberated from the routines and servitudes of organized human activity in order to *be free*. Free for what? Free to see, free to praise, free to understand, free to love. This ideal is easy to describe, much more difficult to realize. Obviously, in reality, the life of a monastic community has many tasks and even certain organized routines so that the monk, in his own little world, lives a social life like everybody else. This social life can become complicated and overactive. And he suffers the same temptations to evasion, to meaninglessness, to bad faith, to restless agitation. But the purpose of the monastic life is to enable a man to face reality in all its naked, disconcerting, possibly drab and disappointing factuality, without excuses, without useless explanations, and without subterfuges.   (CIWA 228)

◆ ◆ ◆

The literature of the Desert Fathers is iconography, rather than character study. It shows us the spiritual radiation of men who are outside history: men who have taken history to themselves and transcended it, who render it transparent, thus showing its inner and secret dimensions. The monastic life, then, is not a mere refusal of history. But for this fruit to mature, there must be true sanctity, and truly *monastic* sanctity. As long as the solitary life is systematically played down, discouraged, and even forbidden, I do not think that even the cenobitic life* will bear its proper fruits.

This is an extreme and radical view, implying the rejection of culture (in order to elevate it also to the "transparent" level), the frank adoption of a life lacking in rational measure, as against the "moderation" and "good sense" of merely ethical norms. But once again, when we consider our monks in the concrete, who of them is able to do this without breaking down?

One of his [Father Paul Evdokimov's] most impressive phrases: *one goes into the desert to vomit up the interior phantom, the doubter, the double.* It is the monk's office to do this for himself and for others, since others are not in a position to do it. The ascesis† of solitude is, then, a deep therapy which has uncovered the ascetic archetype in man. But again, the risk is enormous. When one considers monks in the concrete, one finds them dangerously bound to their double, incapable of "vomiting him out." It is precisely this phantom, this impostor, that dictates the pseudo-asceticism and the contemplative posturing of the misfits.   (CGB 309)

---

*Saint Pachomios of Egypt (d. 346) was the founder of "cenobitic" monasticism (from the Greek *koinos*, "communal"; and *bios*, "life"). The idea was to live a life of contemplation *within a community*.

†*Ascesis* is Greek for "discipline," the practice of denying the self.

◆ ◆ ◆

It is certainly true, then, that this special perspective necessarily implies that the monk will be in some sense critical of the world, of its routines, its confusions, and its sometimes tragic failures to provide other men with lives that are fully sane and human. The monk can and must be open to the world, but at the same time he must be able to get along without a naive and uncritical "secularity" which blandly assumes that everything in the world is at every moment getting better and better for everybody. This critical balance is no doubt difficult to achieve. But it is something which the monk *owes* to *the world.* For the monastic life has a certain prophetic character about it: not that the monk should be able to tell what is about to happen in the Kingdom of God, but in the sense that he is a living witness to the freedom of the sons of God and to the essential difference between that freedom and the spirit of the world. While admitting that God "so loved the world that he gave his only begotten Son" (John 3:16), the monk does not forget that when the Son of God came into the world it did not receive him because it *could* not. It was bound to oppose and reject him.   (CIWA 8–9)

◆ ◆ ◆

The monk is not defined by his task, his usefulness. In a certain sense he is supposed to be "useless" because his mission is not to *do* this or that job but to *be* a man of God. He does not live in order to exercise a specific function: his business is life itself. This means that monasticism aims at the cultivation of a certain *quality* of life, a level of awareness, a depth of consciousness, an area of transcendence and of adoration which are not usually possible in an active secular existence. This does not imply that the secular level is entirely godless and reprobate, or that there can be no real awareness of God in the world. Nor does it mean that worldly life is to be considered wicked or even inferior. But it does mean that more immersion and total absorption in worldly business end by robbing one of a certain necessary perspective. The monk seeks to be free from what William Faulkner called "the same frantic steeplechase toward nothing" which is the essence of "worldliness" everywhere.

(CIWA 7)

◆ ◆ ◆

An abbey is an earthly paradise because it is an earthly purgatory.

(SJ 186)

◆ ◆ ◆

We are living through the greatest crisis in the history of man; and this crisis is centered precisely in the country that has made a fetish out of action and has lost (or perhaps never had) the sense of contemplation. Far from being irrelevant, prayer, meditation and contemplation are of the utmost importance in America today. Unfortunately, it must be admitted that the official contemplative life as it is lived in our monasteries needs a great deal of rethinking, because it is still too closely identified with patterns of thought that were accepted five hundred years ago, but which are completely strange to modern man.

(CIWA 164)

◆ ◆ ◆

The whole illusion of a separate holy existence is a dream. Not that I question the reality of vocation, or of my monastic life: but the conception of "separation from the world" that we have in the monastery too easily presents itself as a complete illusion: the illusion that by making vows we become a different species of being, pseudo-angels, "spiritual men," men of interior life, what have you . . . Thank God, thank God that I *am* like other men, that I am only a man among others. (CGB 140-41)

◆ ◆ ◆

If there is a "problem" for Christianity today, it is the problem of the identification of "Christendom" with certain forms of culture and society, certain political and social structures which for fifteen hundred years have dominated Europe and the West. The first monks were men who, already in the fourth century, began to protest against this identification as a falsehood and a servitude. Fifteen hundred years of European Christendom, in spite of certain definite achievements, have not been an unequivocal glory for Christendom. The time has come for judgment to be passed on this history. I can rejoice in this fact, believing that the judgment will be a liberation of the Christian faith from servitude to and involvement in the structures of the secular world. And that is why I think certain forms of Christian "optimism" are to be taken with reservations, in so far as they lack the genuine eschatological consciousness of the Christian vision, and concentrate upon the naive hope of merely temporal achievements—churches on the moon! (HR 66)

◆ ◆ ◆

The Desert Fathers did, in fact, meet the "problems of their time" in the sense that they were among the few who were ahead of their time, and opened the way for the development of a new man and a new society. They represent what modern philosophers (Jaspers,

Mumford) call the emergence of "axial man,"* the forerunner of the modern personalist man.† The eighteenth and nineteenth centuries with their pragmatic individualism degraded and corrupted the psychological heritage of axial man with its debt to the Desert Fathers and other contemplatives, and prepared the way for the great regression to the herd mentality that is taking place now.   (WOD 4)

FAITH

The man who does not permit his spirit to be beaten down and upset by dryness and helplessness, but who lets God lead him peacefully through the wilderness, and desires no other support or guidance than that of pure faith and trust in God alone, will be brought to the Promised Land.   (NS 239)

◆ ◆ ◆

The religious problem of the twentieth century is not understandable if we regard it only as a problem of Unbelievers and of atheists.

---

*A number of observers have noted that in the sixth century before Christ a new type of thinking arose in five different parts of the Eurasian continent at the same time: Confucius and Lao-tzu emerged in China, Gautama Buddha in India, and Zoroaster in Persia. Thales and Pythagoras were founding Greek philosophy, while the prophetic movement in Israel reached a climax in Second Isaiah. What distinguished these new "axial men" was the role rationality played in the structure of their existence. They increasingly came to be at home in the world of rational consciousness and estranged from the mythical world that still dominated most of human existence. Great spiritual teachers and philosophers emerged who could destroy the power of the mythical world, and this drastic break with the consciousness of the past constituted the *axial* period. The cultures and religions this new existence gave rise to are the *axial* cultures and religions, which still dominate world culture and religion.

†"Personalist man," according to Jaspers, evolved out of *axial man* and represents the next phase of civilization, whose structure and spirit are specifically directed toward the development of all individuals as persons with a maximum of initiative, responsibility, and spiritual life.

It is also and perhaps chiefly a problem of Believers. The faith that has grown cold is not only the faith that the Unbeliever has lost but the faith that the Believer has kept. This faith has too often become rigid, or complex, sentimental, foolish, or impertinent. It has lost itself in imaginings and unrealities, dispersed itself in pontifical and organizational routines, or evaporated in activism and loose talk.

The most hopeful sign of religious renewal is the authentic sincerity and openness with which some Believers are beginning to recognize this. At the very moment when it would seem that they had to gather for a fanatical last-ditch stand, these Believers are dropping their defensiveness, their defiance and their mistrust. They are realizing that a faith that is afraid of other people is no faith at all.

(FAV 213–14)

◆ ◆ ◆

Absurdity [is] the anguish of realizing that underneath the apparently logical pattern of a more or less "well organized" and rational life, there lies an abyss of irrationality, confusion, pointlessness, and indeed of apparent chaos. This is what immediately impresses itself upon the man who has renounced diversion. It cannot be otherwise: for in renouncing diversion, he renounces the seemingly harmless pleasure of building a tight, self-contained illusion about himself and his little world. He accepts the difficulty of facing the million things in his life which are incomprehensible instead of simply ignoring them. Incidentally it is only when the apparent absurdity of life is faced in all truth that faith really becomes possible. Otherwise, faith tends to be a kind of diversion, a spiritual amusement, in which one gathers up accepted, conventional formulas and arranges them in the approved mental patterns, without bothering to investigate their meaning, or asking if they have any practical consequences in one's life.   (DQ 179–80)

◆ ◆ ◆

Self-confidence is a precious natural gift, a sign of health. But it is not the same thing as faith. Faith is much deeper, and it must be deep enough to subsist when we are weak, when we are sick, when our self-confidence is gone, when our self-respect is gone. I do not mean that faith *only* functions when we are otherwise in a state of collapse. But true faith must be able to go on even when everything else is taken away from us. Only a humble man is able to accept faith on these terms, so completely without reservation that he is glad of it in its pure state, and welcomes it happily even when nothing else comes with it, and when everything else is taken away.

(NS 187)

◆ ◆ ◆

For some "faithful"—and for unbelievers too—"faith" seems to be a kind of drunkenness, an anesthetic, that keeps you from realizing and believing that anything can ever go wrong. Such faith can be immersed in a world of violence and make no objection: the violence is perfectly all right. It is quite normal—unless of course it happens to be exercised by Negroes. Then it must be put down instantly by superior force. The drunkenness of this kind of faith—whether in a religious message or merely in a political ideology—enables us to go through life without seeing that our own violence is a disaster and that the overwhelming force by which we seek to assert ourselves and our own self-interest may be our ruin.

Is faith a narcotic dream in a world of heavily-armed robbers, or is it an awakening?

Is faith a convenient nightmare in which we are attacked and obliged to destroy our attackers?

What if we awaken to discover that *we* are the robbers, and our destruction comes from the root of hate in ourselves?   (FAV IX-X)

◆ ◆ ◆

How many people there are in the world of today who have "lost their faith" along with the vain hopes and illusions of their childhood. What they called "faith" was just one among all the other illusions. They placed all their hope in a certain sense of spiritual peace, of comfort, of interior equilibrium, of self-respect. Then when they began to struggle with the real difficulties and burdens of mature life, when they became aware of their own weakness, they lost their peace, they let go of their precious self-respect, and it became impossible for them to "believe." That is to say it became impossible for them to comfort themselves, to reassure themselves, with the images and concepts that they found reassuring in childhood.

Place no hope in the feeling of assurance, in spiritual comfort. You may well have to get along without this.   (NS 186-87)

◆ ◆ ◆

Indeed, the truth that many people never understand, until it is too late, is that the more you try to avoid suffering, the more you suffer, because smaller and more insignificant things begin to torture you, in proportion to your fear of being hurt. The one who does most to avoid suffering is, in the end, the one who suffers most: and his suffering comes to him from things so little and so trivial that one can say that it is no longer objective at all. It is his own existence, his own being, that is at once the subject and the source of his pain, and his very existence and consciousness is his greatest torture. This is another of the great perversions by which the devil uses our philosophies to turn our whole nature inside out, and eviscerate all our capacities for good, turning them against ourselves.   (ssm 82–83)

◆ ◆ ◆

In getting the best of our secret attachments—ones which we cannot see because they are principles of spiritual blindness—our own initiative is almost always useless. We need to leave the initiative in the hands of God working in our souls either directly in the night of aridity and suffering, or through events and other men.

This is where so many holy people break down and go to pieces. As soon as they reach the point where they can no longer see the way and guide themselves by their own light, they refuse to go any further. They have no confidence in anyone except themselves. Their faith is largely an emotional illusion. It is rooted in their feelings, in their physique, in their temperament. It is a kind of natural optimism that is stimulated by moral activity and warmed by the approval of other men. If people oppose it, this kind of faith still finds refuge in self-complacency.

But when the time comes to enter the darkness in which we are naked and helpless and alone; in which we see the insufficiency of our greatest strength and the hollowness of our strongest virtues; in which we have nothing of our own to rely on, and nothing in our nature to support us, and nothing in the world to guide us or give us light—then we find out whether or not we live by faith.

It is in this darkness, when there is nothing left in us that can please or comfort our own minds, when we seem to be useless and worthy of all contempt, when we seem to have failed, when we seem to be destroyed and devoured, it is then that the deep and secret selfishness that is too close for us to identify is stripped away from our souls. It is in this darkness that we find true liberty. It is in this abandonment that we are made strong. This is the night which empties us and makes us pure. (NS 257–58)

◆　◆　◆

Faith is primarily intellectual assent. But if it were only that and nothing more, if it were only the "argument of what does not appear," it would not be complete. It has to be something more than assent of the mind. It is also a grasp, a contact, a communion of wills, "the substance of things hoped for." By faith one not only consents to propositions revealed by God, one not only attains to truth in a way that intelligence and reason alone cannot do, but one assents to God Himself. One *receives* God. One says "yes" not merely to a statement *about* God, but to the Invisible, Infinite God Himself. . . .

Faith, then, is not just the grim determination to cling to a certain form of words, no matter what may happen—though we must certainly be prepared to defend our creed with our life. But above all faith is the opening of the inward eye, the eye of the heart, to be filled with the presence of the Divine light. (NS 128–30)

◆　◆　◆

If we are not humble, we tend to demand that faith must also bring with it good health, peace of mind, good luck, success in business, popularity, world peace, and every other good thing we can imagine. And it is true that God can give us all these good things if He wants to. But they are of no importance compared with faith, which is essential. If we insist on other things as the price of our believing, we tend by that very fact to undermine our own belief. I do not think it would be an act of mercy on God's part simply to let us get away with this! (NS 187–88)

◆ ◆ ◆

Be careful of every vain hope: it is in reality a temptation to despair. It may seem very real, very substantial. You may come to depend far too much on this apparent solidity of what you think is soon to be yours. You may make your whole spiritual life, your very faith itself, depend on this illusory promise. Then, when it dissolves into air, everything else dissolves along with it. Your whole spiritual life slips away between your fingers and you are left with nothing.

In reality, this could be a good thing, and we should be able to regard it as a good thing, if only we could fall back on the substantiality of pure and obscure faith, which cannot deceive us. But our faith is weak. Indeed, too often the weakest thing about our faith is the illusion that our faith is strong, when the "strength" we feel is only the intensity of emotion or of sentiment, which has nothing to do with real faith. (NS 186)

CHARITY

Charity is a love for God which respects the need that other men have for Him. Therefore, charity alone can give us the power and the delicacy to love others without defiling their loneliness which is their need and their salvation. (NM 244)

◆ ◆ ◆

This is the great paradox of charity: that unless we are selfish enough to desire to become perfectly unselfish, we have not charity. And unless we love ourselves enough to seek perfect happiness in the total forgetfulness of ourselves, we will never find happiness.

Charity is a self-interest which seeks fulfillment in the renunciation of all its interests. (BIW 102)

◆ ◆ ◆

Charity is created and strengthened within us by the action of the Holy Spirit—most of all in times of trial and sacrifice, because it is then that we are pressed and compelled, by circumstances, to make heroic choices that confirm our union with Christ, and teach us to know Him as He is. For Christ without the Cross is not our Christ. True, He is now the risen Christ. He knows no suffering. He "dieth now no more." But He has wounds. Even though they be glorious, they are wounds. (BIW 90)

◆ ◆ ◆

It is easy enough to tell the poor to accept their poverty as God's will when you yourself have warm clothes and plenty of food and medical care and a roof over your head and no worry about the rent. But if you want them to believe you—try to share some of their poverty and see if you accept it as God's will yourself! (NS 179)

◆ ◆ ◆

In the economy of divine charity we have only as much as we give. But we are called upon to give as much as we have, and more: as much as we are. So the measure of our love is theoretically without limit. The more we desire to give ourselves in charity, the more charity we will have to give. And the more we give the more truly we shall be. For the Lord endows us with a being proportionate to the giving for which we are destined.

Charity is the life and the riches of His Kingdom, and those are greatest in it who are least: that is, who have kept nothing for themselves, retaining nothing but their desire to give.

He who tries to retain what he is and what he has, and keep it for himself, buries his talent. When the Lord comes in judgment, this servant is found to have no more than he had at the beginning. But those who have made themselves less, by giving away what they had, shall be found both to be and to have more than they had. And to him who has most shall be given that which the unprofitable servant kept for himself. (NM 164)

HUMILITY

The value of our activity depends almost entirely on the humility to accept ourselves as we are. The reason why we do things so badly is that we are not content to do what we can.

We insist on doing what is not asked of us, because we want to taste the success that belongs to somebody else.

We never discover what it is like to make a success of our own work, because we do not want to undertake any work that is merely proportionate to our powers.

Who is willing to be satisfied with a job that expresses all his limitations? He will accept such work only as a "means of livelihood" while he waits to discover his "true vocation." The world is full of unsuccessful businessmen who still secretly believe they were meant to be artists or writers or actors in the movies. (NM 124)

◆ ◆ ◆

A man who is not stripped and poor and naked within his own soul will unconsciously tend to do the works he has to do for his own sake rather than for the glory of God. He will be virtuous not because he loves God's will but because he wants to admire his own virtues. But every moment of the day will bring him some frustration that will make him bitter and impatient and in his impatience he will be discovered.

He has planned to do spectacular things. He cannot conceive himself without a halo. And when the events of his daily life keep reminding him of his own insignificance and mediocrity, he is ashamed, and his pride refuses to swallow a truth at which no sane man should be surprised. (NS 58-59)

◆ ◆ ◆

We cannot avoid missing the point of almost everything we do. But what of it? Life is not a matter of getting something out of everything. Life itself is imperfect. All created beings begin to die as soon as they begin to live, and no one expects any one of them to become absolutely perfect, still less to stay that way. Each individual thing is only a sketch of the specific perfection planned for its kind. Why should we ask it to be anything more?

If we are too anxious to find absolute perfection in created things we cease to look for perfection where alone it can be found: in God. The secret of the imperfection of all things, of their inconstancy, their fragility, their falling into nothingness, is that they are only a shadowy expression of the one Being from Whom they receive their being. If they were absolutely perfect and changeless in themselves, they would fail in their vocation, which is to give glory to God by their contingency. (NM 128-29)

◆ ◆ ◆

One who is content with what he has, and who accepts the fact that he inevitably misses very much in life, is far better off than one who has much more but who worries about all he may be missing. For we cannot make the best of what we are, if our hearts are always divided between what we are and what we are not. . . .

We cannot be happy if we expect to live all the time at the highest peak of intensity. Happiness is not a matter of intensity but of balance and order and rhythm and harmony. . . .

Let us, therefore, learn to pass from one imperfect activity to another without worrying too much about what we are missing.

(NM 127–28)

◆　◆　◆

When one has too many answers, and when one joins a chorus of others chanting the same slogans, there is, it seems to me, a danger that one is trying to evade the loneliness of a conscience that realizes itself to be in an inescapably evil situation. We are all under judgment. None of us is free from contamination. Our choice is not that of being pure and whole at the mere cost of formulating a just and honest opinion. Mere commitment to a decent program of action does not lift the curse. Our real choice is between being like Job, who *knew* he was stricken, and Job's friends who did not know that they were stricken too—though less obviously than he. (So they had answers!) (FAV 145–46)

◆　◆　◆

The fruitfulness of our life depends in large measure on our ability to doubt our own words and to question the value of our own work. The man who completely trusts his own estimate of himself is doomed to sterility. All he asks of any act he performs is that it be *his* act. If it is performed by him, it must be good. All words spoken by him must be infallible. The car he has just bought is the best for its price, for no other reason than that he is the one who has bought it. He seeks no other fruit than this, and therefore he generally gets no other.

If we believe ourselves in part, we may be right about ourselves. If we are completely taken in by our own disguise, we cannot help being wrong. (NM 124–25)

◆　◆　◆

What we need is the gift of God which makes us able to find in ourselves not just ourselves but Him: and then our nothingness becomes His all. This is not possible without the liberation effected by compunction and humility. It requires not talent, not mere insight, but *sorrow*, pouring itself out in *love* and *trust*. (CQR 214)

◆　◆　◆

Despair is the absolute extreme of self-love. It is reached when a man deliberately turns his back on all help from anyone else in order to taste the rotten luxury of knowing himself to be lost.

In every man there is hidden some root of despair because in every man there is pride that vegetates and springs weeds and rank flowers of self-pity as soon as our own resources fail us. But because our own resources inevitably fail us, we are all more or less subject to discouragement and to despair.

Despair is the ultimate development of a pride so great and so stiff-necked that it selects the absolute misery of damnation rather than accept happiness from the hands of God and thereby acknowledge that He is above us and that we are not capable of fulfilling our destiny by ourselves.

But the man who is truly humble cannot despair, because in the humble man there is no longer any such thing as self-pity. (NS 180)

◆ ◆ ◆

Only the man who has had to face despair is really convinced that he needs mercy. Those who do not want mercy never seek it. It is better to find God on the threshold of despair than to risk our lives in a complacency that has never felt the need of forgiveness. A life that is without problems may literally be more hopeless than one that always verges on despair. (NM 21–22)

◆ ◆ ◆

God is more glorified by a man who uses the good things of this life in simplicity and with gratitude than by the nervous asceticism of someone who is agitated about every detail of his self-denial. The former uses good things and thinks of God. The latter is afraid of good things, and consequently cannot use them properly. He is terrified of the pleasure God has put in things, and in his terror thinks only of himself. He imagines God has placed all the good things of the world before him like bait in a trap. He worries at all times about his own "perfection." His struggle for perfection becomes a kind of battle of wits with the Creator who made all things good. The very goodness of creatures becomes a threat to the purity of this virtuous one, who would like to abstain from everything. But he cannot. He is human, like the rest of men, and must make use like them of food and drink and sleep. Like them he must see the sky, and love, in spite of oneself, the light of the sun! Every feeling of pleasure fills him with a sense of guilt. It has besmirched his own adored perfection. Strange that people like this should enter monasteries, which have no other reason for existing than the love of God! (NM 114–15)

◆ ◆ ◆

When it comes to fighting the deep and unconscious habits of attachment which we can hardly dig up and recognize, all our meditations, self-examinations, resolutions and planned campaigns may not only be ineffective but may even sometimes lend assistance to our enemies. Because it may easily happen that our resolutions are dictated by the vice we need to get rid of. And so the proud man resolves to fast more and punish his flesh more because he wants to make himself feel like an athlete: his fasts and disciplines are imposed on him by his own vanity, and they strengthen the thing in him that most needs to be killed. (NS 257)

◆ ◆ ◆

We must never overlook the fact that the message of the Bible is above all a message preached to the poor, the burdened, the oppressed, the underprivileged. (OTB 51)

◆ ◆ ◆

Asceticism is utterly useless if it turns us into freaks. The cornerstone of all asceticism is humility, and Christian humility is first of all a matter of supernatural common sense. It teaches us to take ourselves as we are, instead of pretending (as pride would have us imagine) that we are something better than we are. If we really know ourselves, we quietly take our proper place in the order designed by God. And so supernatural humility adds much to our human dignity by integrating us into the society of other men and placing us in our right relation to them and to God. Pride makes us artificial, and humility makes us real. (NM 113)

◆ ◆ ◆

When humility delivers a man from attachment to his own works and his own reputation, he discovers that perfect joy is possible only when we have completely forgotten ourselves. And it is only when we pay no more attention to our own deeds and our own reputation and our own excellence that we are at last completely free to serve God in perfection for His own sake alone.   (NS 58)

◆　◆　◆

If you were truly humble you would not bother about yourself at all. Why should you? You would only be concerned with God and with His will and with the objective order of things and values as they are, and not as your selfishness wants them to be. Consequently you would have no more illusions to defend. Your movements would be free. You would not need to be hampered with excuses which are really only framed to defend you against the accusation of pride—as if your humility depended on what other people thought of you!

(NS 189–90)

◆　◆　◆

A humble man can do great things with an uncommon perfection because he is no longer concerned about incidentals, like his own interests and his own reputation, and therefore he no longer needs to waste his efforts in defending them.

For a humble man is not afraid of failure. In fact, he is not afraid of anything, even of himself, since perfect humility implies perfect confidence in the power of God before Whom no other power has any meaning and for Whom there is no such thing as an obstacle.

Humility is the surest sign of strength.   (NS 190)

◆　◆　◆

Teach me to bear a humility which shows me, without ceasing, that I am a liar and a fraud and that, even though this is so, I have an obligation to strive after truth, to be as true as I can, even though I will inevitably find all my truth half poisoned with deceit. This is the terrible thing about humility: that it is never fully successful. If only it were possible to be completely humble on this earth. But no, that is the trouble: You, Lord, were humble. But our humility consists in being proud and knowing all about it, and being crushed by the unbearable weight of it, and to be able to do so little about it.

How stern You are in Your mercy, and yet You must be. Your mercy has to be just because Your Truth has to be True. How stern You are, nevertheless, in Your mercy: for the more we struggle to be true, the more we discover our falsity. Is it merciful of Your light to bring us, inexorably, to despair?

No—it is not to despair that You bring me but to humility. For true humility is, in a way, a very real despair: despair of myself, in order that I may hope entirely in You.

What man can bear to fall into such darkness? (TIS 66)

VOCATION

There is only one vocation. Whether you teach or live in the cloister or nurse the sick, whether you are in religion or out of it, married or single, no matter who you are or what you are, you are called to the summit of perfection: you are called to a deep interior life perhaps even to mystical prayer, and to pass the fruits of your contemplation on to others. And if you cannot do so by word, then by example. (SSM 419)

◆ ◆ ◆

The fulfillment of every individual vocation demands not only the renouncement of what is evil in itself, but also *of all the precise goods that are not willed for us by God.*

It takes exceptional courage and integrity to make such a sacrifice. We cannot do it unless we are really seeking to do the will of God for His sake alone. The man who is content to keep from disobeying God, and to satisfy his own desires wherever there is nothing to prevent him from doing so, may indeed lead a life that is not evil: but his life will remain a sad confusion of truth and falsity and he will never have the spiritual vision to tell one clearly from the other. He will never fully live up to his vocation. (NM 137)

◆　◆　◆

The remarkable thing about St. Francis is that in his sacrifice of everything he had also sacrificed all the "vocations" in a limited sense of the word. After having been edified for centuries by all the various branches of the Franciscan religious family, we are surprised to think that St. Francis started out on the roads of Umbria without the slightest idea that he had a "Franciscan vocation." And in fact he did not. He had thrown all vocations to the winds together with his clothes and other possessions. He did not think of himself as an apostle, but as a tramp. He certainly did not look upon himself as a monk: if he had wanted to be a monk, he would have found plenty of monasteries to enter. He evidently did not go around conscious of the fact that he was a "contemplative." Nor was he worried by comparisons between the active and contemplative lives. Yet he led both at the same time, and with the highest perfection. No good work was alien to him—no work of mercy, whether corporal or spiritual, that did not have a place in his beautiful life! His freedom embraced everything. (NM 161)

◆　◆　◆

Our vocation is not simply to *be,* but to work together with God in the creation of our own life, our own identity, our own destiny. We are free beings and sons of God. This means to say that we should not passively exist, but actively participate in His creative freedom, in our own lives, and in the lives of others, by choosing the truth. To put it better, we are even called to share with God the work of *creating* the truth of our identity. We can evade this responsibility by playing with masks, and this pleases us because it can appear at times to be a free and creative way of living. It is quite easy, it seems, to please everyone. But in the long run the cost and the sorrow come very high. To work out our own identity in God, which the Bible calls "working out our salvation," is a labor that requires sacrifice and anguish, risk and many tears. It demands close attention to reality at every moment, and great fidelity to God as He reveals Himself, obscurely, in the mystery of each new situation.   (NS 32)

◆ ◆ ◆

The blind spiritual instinct that tells us obscurely that our own lives have a particular importance and purpose, and which urges us to find out our vocation, seeks in so doing to bring us to a decision that will dedicate our lives irrevocably to their true purpose. The man who loses this sense of his own personal destiny, and who renounces all hope of having any kind of vocation in life has either lost all hope of happiness or else has entered upon some mysterious vocation that God alone can understand.   (NM 140)

◆ ◆ ◆

Gratitude and confidence and freedom from ourselves: these are signs that we have found our vocation and are living up to it even though everything else may seem to have gone wrong. They give us peace in any suffering. They teach us to laugh at despair. And we may have to.   (NM 140)

GOD

At the center of our being is a point of nothingness which is untouched by sin and by illusion, a point of pure truth, a point or spark which belongs entirely to God, which is never at our disposal, from which God disposes of our lives, which is inaccessible to the fantasies of our own mind or the brutalities of our own will. This little point of nothingness and of *absolute poverty* is the pure glory of God in us. It is so to speak His name written in us, as our poverty, as our indigence, as our dependence, as our sonship. It is like a pure diamond, blazing with the invisible light of heaven. It is in everybody, and if we could see it we would see these billions of points of light coming together in the face and blaze of a sun that would make all the darkness and cruelty of life vanish completely. . . . I have no program for this seeing. It is only given. But the gate of heaven is everywhere.   (CGB 142)

◆　◆　◆

In order to find God in ourselves, we must stop looking at ourselves, stop checking and verifying ourselves in the mirror of our own futility, and be content to *be* in Him and to do whatever He wills, according to our limitations, judging our acts not in the light of our own illusions, but in the light of His reality which is all around us in the things and people we live with.   (NM 120)

◆　◆　◆

We must be saved from immersion in the sea of lies and passions which is called "the world." And we must be saved above all from that abyss of confusion and absurdity which is our own worldly self. The person must be rescued from the individual. The free son of God must be saved from the conformist slave of fantasy, passion and convention. The creative and mysterious inner self must be delivered from the wasteful, hedonistic and destructive ego that seeks only to cover itself with disguises.

To be "lost" is to be left to the arbitrariness and pretenses of the contingent ego, the smoke-self that must inevitably vanish. To be "saved" is to return to one's inviolate and eternal reality and to live in God. (NS 38)

◆　◆　◆

If we ask the Bible, as we ultimately must when we enter into serious dialog with it: "Who is this Father? What is meant by Father? Show us the Father?" we in our turn are asked in effect: "Who are *you* who seek to know 'the Father' and what do you think you are seeking anyway?" And we are told: Find yourself in love of your brother as if he were Christ (since in fact he 'is Christ') and you will know the Father (see John 14:8–17). That is to say: if you live for *others* you will have an intimate personal knowledge of the love that rises up in you out of a ground that lies beyond your own freedom and your own inclination, and yet is present as the very core of your own free and personal identity. Penetrating to that inner ground of love you at last find your true self. (OTB 33)

◆　◆　◆

People who know nothing of God and whose lives are centered on themselves, imagine that they can only find themselves by asserting their own desires and ambitions and appetites in a struggle with the rest of the world. They try to become real by imposing themselves on other people, by appropriating for themselves some share of the limited supply of created goods and thus emphasizing the difference between themselves and the other men who have less than they, or nothing at all.

They can only conceive one way of becoming real: cutting themselves off from other people and building a barrier of contrast and distinction between themselves and other men. They do not know that reality is to be sought not in division but in unity, for we are "members one of another." (NS 47–48)

◆　◆　◆

Fickleness and indecision are signs of self-love.

If you can never make up your mind what God wills for you, but are always veering from one opinion to another, from one practice to another, from one method to another, it may be an indication that you are trying to get around God's will and do your own with a quiet conscience.

As soon as God gets you in one monastery you want to be in another.

As soon as you taste one way of prayer, you want to try another. You are always making resolutions and breaking them by counter-resolutions. You ask your confessor and do not remember the answers. Before you finish one book you begin another, and with every book you read you change the whole plan of your interior life.

Soon you will have no interior life at all. Your whole existence will be a patchwork of confused desires and daydreams and velleities in which you do nothing except defeat the work of grace: for all this is an elaborate subconscious device of your nature to resist God,

Whose work in your soul demands the sacrifice of all that you desire and delight in, and, indeed, of all that you are.

So keep still, and let Him do some work.

This is what it means to renounce not only pleasures and possessions, but even your own self. (NS 260–61)

◆ ◆ ◆

God approaches our minds by receding from them. We can never fully know Him if we think of Him as an object of capture, to be fenced in by the enclosure of our own ideas.

We know Him better after our minds have let Him go.

The Lord travels in all directions at once.

The Lord arrives from all directions at once.

Wherever we are, we find that He has just departed.

Wherever we go, we discover that He has just arrived before us.

Our rest can be neither in the beginning of this pursuit, nor in the pursuit itself, nor in its apparent end. For the true end, which is Heaven, is an end without end. It is a totally new dimension, in which we come to rest in the secret that He must arrive at the moment of His departure; His arrival is at every moment and His departure is not fixed in time. (NM 239)

◆ ◆ ◆

It is not that someone else is preventing you from living happily; you yourself do not know what you want. Rather than admit this, you pretend that someone is keeping you from exercising your liberty. Who is this? It is you yourself.

But as long as you pretend to live in pure autonomy, as your own master, without even a god to rule you, you will inevitably live as the servant of another man or as the alienated member of an organization. Paradoxically it is the acceptance of God that makes you free and delivers you from human tyranny, for when you serve Him you are no longer permitted to alienate your spirit in human servitude. God did not *invite* the Children of Israel to leave the slavery of Egypt: He *commanded* them to do so. (NS 110)

◆ ◆ ◆

The man whose view of life is purely secular, hates himself interiorly, while seeming to love himself. He hates himself in the sense that he cannot stand to be "with" or "by" himself. And because he hates himself, he also tends to hate God, because he cannot abide the inner loneliness which must be suffered and accepted, before God can be found. His rebellion against his own inner loneliness and poverty turns into pride. Pride is the fixation of the interior self upon itself, and the rejection of all other elements in the self for which it is incapable of assuming responsibility. This includes the rejection of the inmost self, with its apparent emptiness, its indefiniteness, and its general character as that which is dark and unknown. Pride is then a false and evasive self-realization which is in actual fact no realization at all, but only the fabrication of an illusory image. The effort which must then be put into the protection and substantiation of this illusion gives an appearance of strength. But in reality, this fixation upon what does not exist merely exhausts and ruins our being.

There is a subtle but inescapable connection between the "sacred" attitude and the acceptance of one's inmost self. The movement of recognition which accepts our own obscure and unknown self produces the sensation of a "numinous" presence within us. This sacred awe is no mere magic illusion but the real expression of a release of spiritual energy, testifying to our own interior reunion and reconciliation with that which is deepest in us, and, through the inner self, with the transcendent and invisible power of God. This implies humility, or the full acceptance of all that we have tended to reject and ignore in ourselves. The inner self is "purified" by the acknowledgment of sin, not precisely because the inner self is the seat of sin, but because both our sinfulness and our interiority tend to be rejected in one and the same movement by the exterior self, and relegated to the same darkness, so that when the inner self is brought back to light, sin emerges and is liquidated by the assuming of responsibility and by sorrow. (CQR 214-15)

◆ ◆ ◆

God gives us freedom to make our own lives within the situation which is the gift of His love to us, and by means of the power His love grants us. But we feel guilty about it. We are quite capable of being happy in the life He has provided for us, in which we can contentedly make our own way, helped by His grace. We are ashamed to do so. For we need one thing more than happiness: we need approval. And the need for approval destroys our capacity for happiness. "How can you believe, who seek glory one from another?"* (CGB 84)

◆ ◆ ◆

To believe in suffering is pride: but to suffer, believing in God, is humility. For pride may tell us that we are strong enough to suffer, that suffering is good for us because we are good. Humility tells us that suffering is an evil which we must always expect to find in our lives because of the evil that is in ourselves. But faith also knows that the mercy of God is given to those who seek Him in suffering,

*John 5:44.

and that by His grace we can overcome evil with good. Suffering, then, becomes good by accident, by the good that it enables us to receive more abundantly from the mercy of God. It does not make us good by itself, but it enables us to make ourselves better than we are. Thus, what we consecrate to God in suffering is not our suffering but our *selves*.   (NM 78)

◆ ◆ ◆

At no time in the spiritual life is it more necessary to be completely docile and subject to the most delicate movements of God's will and His grace than when you try to share the knowledge of His love with other men. It is much better to be so diffident that you risk not sharing it with them at all, than to throw it all away by trying to give it to other people before you have received it yourself. The contemplative who tries to preach contemplation before he himself really knows what it is, will prevent both himself and others from finding the true path to God's peace.

In the first place he will substitute his own natural enthusiasm and imagination and poetry for the reality of the light that is in him, and he will become absorbed in the business of communicating something that is practically incommunicable: and although there is some benefit in this even for his own soul (for it is a kind of meditation on the interior life and on God) still he runs the risk of being drawn away from the simple light and silence in which God is known without words and concepts, and losing himself in reasoning and language and metaphor.   (NS 270)

◆ ◆ ◆

Cartesian thought began with an attempt to reach God as object by starting from the thinking self.* But when God becomes object, he

*Named after the French philosopher René Descartes (1596–1650), Cartesian thought refers to

sooner or later "dies," because God as object is ultimately unthinkable. God as object is not only a mere abstract concept, but one
which contains so many internal contradictions that it becomes entirely nonnegotiable except when it is hardened into an idol that is
maintained in existence by a sheer act of will. For a long time man
continued to be capable of this willfulness: but now the effort has
become exhausting and many Christians have realized it to be futile.
Relaxing the effort, they have let go the "God-object" which their
fathers and grandfathers still hoped to manipulate for their own
ends. Their weariness has accounted for the element of resentment
which made this a conscious "murder" of the deity. Liberated from
the strain of willfully maintaining an object-God in existence, the
Cartesian consciousness remains none the less imprisoned in itself.
Hence the need to break out of itself and to meet "the other" in
"encounter," "openness," "fellowship," "communion."   (z&b 23)

◆　◆　◆

People seem to think that it is in some way a proof that no merciful
God exists, if we have so many wars. On the contrary consider how
in spite of centuries of sin and greed and lust and cruelty and hatred
and avarice and oppression and injustice, spawned and bred by the
free wills of men, the human race can still recover, each time, and
can still produce men and women who overcome evil with good,
hatred with love, greed with charity, lust and cruelty with sanctity.
How could all this be possible without the merciful love of God,
pouring out His grace upon us? Can there be any doubt where wars
come from and where peace comes from, when the children of this

---

the line of inquiry that extends the mathematical method into all realms of knowledge in the
search for certainty. Beginning with universal doubt, Descartes believed that the only thing
that could not be doubted was his own thinking, hence the famous Cartesian maxim "I think;
therefore, I am."

world, excluding God from their peace conferences, only manage to bring about greater and greater wars the more they talk about peace?

(SSM 128)

◆ ◆ ◆

Of all the things and all the happenings that proclaim God's will to the world, only very few are capable of being interpreted by men. And of these few, fewer still find a capable interpreter. So that the mystery of God's will is made doubly mysterious by the signs that veil it from our eyes. To know anything at all of God's will we have to participate, in some manner, in the vision of the prophets: men who were always alive to the divine light concealed in the opacity of things and events, and who sometimes saw glimpses of that light where other men saw nothing but ordinary happenings.   (NM 62)

◆ ◆ ◆

The self is not its own center and does not orbit around itself; it is centered on God, the one center of all, which is "everywhere and nowhere." In whom all are encountered, from whom all proceed. Thus from the very start this consciousness is disposed to encounter "the other" with whom it is already united anyway "in God."

(Z&B 24)

◆ ◆ ◆

Hope not because you think you can be good, but because God loves us irrespective of our merits and whatever is good in us comes from His love, not from our own doing.   (MJ 172)

◆ ◆ ◆

He is closer to us than we are to ourselves, although we do not see him.

Whoever seeks to catch Him and hold Him loses Him. He is like the wind that blows where it pleases. You who love Him must love Him as arriving from where you do not know and as going where you do not know. Your spirit must seek to be as clean and as free as His own Spirit, in order to follow Him wherever He goes. Who are we to call ourselves either clean or free, unless He makes us so?

If He should teach us how to follow Him into the wilderness of His own freedom, we will no longer know where we are, because we are with Him Who is everywhere and nowhere at the same time.

Those who love only His apparent presence cannot follow the Lord wherever He goes. They do not love Him perfectly if they do not allow Him to be absent. They do not respect His liberty to do as He pleases. They think their prayers have made them able to command Him, and to subject His will to their own. They live on the level of magic rather than on the level of religion.

Only those men are never separated from the Lord who never question His right to separate Himself from them. They never lose Him because they always realize they never deserve to find Him, and that in spite of their unworthiness they have already found Him.

For He has first found them, and will not let them go. (NM 238)

PART FOUR

Love in Action

Dostoyevsky once wrote, "Love in action is a harsh and dreadful thing compared to love in dreams. Love in dreams is greedy for immediate action, rapidly performed and in the sight of all."

Merton's deep experiential awareness of just how hard it is to live a real Christian life, coupled with his ability to describe that labor, made him one of this century's most trustworthy spiritual guides.

This section explores the challenges and pitfalls of living a life of active love.

TOWARD A THEOLOGY OF LOVE

The one thing necessary is a true interior and spiritual life, true growth, on my own, in depth in a new direction. Whatever new direction God opens up for me. My job is to press forward, to grow interiorly, to pray, to break away from attachments and to defy fears, to grow in faith, which has its own solitude, to seek an entirely new perspective and new dimension in my life. To open up new horizons at any cost, to desire this and let the Holy Spirit take care of the rest. But really to desire this and *work* for it.   (IM 144)

◆　◆　◆

A theology of love cannot afford to be sentimental. It cannot afford to preach edifying generalities about charity, while identifying "peace" with mere established power and legalized violence against the oppressed. A theology of love cannot be allowed merely to serve the interests of the rich and powerful, justifying their wars, their violence and their bombs, while exhorting the poor and underprivileged to practice patience, meekness, longsuffering and to solve their problems, if at all, non-violently.

The theology of love must seek to deal realistically with the evil and injustice in the world, and not merely to compromise with them. Such a theology will have to take note of the ambiguous realities of politics, without embracing the specious myth of a "realism" that merely justifies force in the service of established power. Theology does not exist merely to appease the already too untroubled conscience of the powerful and the established. A theology of love may also conceivably turn out to be a theology of revolution. In any case, it is a theology of *resistance,* a refusal of the evil that reduces a brother to homicidal desperation. (FAV 8–9)

◆ ◆ ◆

All men seek peace first of all with themselves. That is necessary, because we do not naturally find rest even in our own being. We have to learn to commune with ourselves before we can communicate with other men and with God. A man who is not at peace with himself necessarily projects his interior fighting into the society of those he lives with, and spreads a contagion of conflict all around him. Even when he tries to do good to others his efforts are hopeless, since he does not know how to do good to himself. In moments of wildest idealism he may take it into his head to make other people happy: and in doing so he will overwhelm them with his own unhappiness. He seeks to find himself somehow in the work of making others happy. Therefore he throws himself into the work. As a result he gets out of the work all that he put into it: his own confusion, his own disintegration, his own unhappiness. (NM 120–21)

◆ ◆ ◆

Since I am a man, my destiny depends on my human behavior: that is to say upon my decisions. I must first of all appreciate this fact and weigh the risks and difficulties it entails. I must therefore know myself, and know both the good and the evil that are in me. It will not do to know only one and not the other: only the good, or only the evil. I must then be able to love the life God has given me, living it fully and fruitfully, and making good use even of the evil that is in it. Why should I love an ideal good in such a way that my life becomes more deeply embedded in misery and evil? (CGB 81)

◆ ◆ ◆

He who attempts to act and do things for others or for the world without deepening his own self-understanding, freedom, integrity and capacity to love, will not have anything to give others. He will communicate to them nothing but the contagion of his own obsessions, his aggressiveness, his ego-centered ambitions, his delusions about ends and means, his doctrinaire prejudices and ideas. There is nothing more tragic in the modern world than the misuse of power and action to which men are driven by their own Faustian misunderstandings and misapprehensions. We have more power at our disposal today than we have ever had, and yet we are more alienated and estranged from the inner ground of meaning and of love than we have ever been. (CIWA 164)

◆ ◆ ◆

The basic and most fundamental problem of the spiritual life is this acceptance of our hidden and dark self, with which we tend to identify all the evil that is in us. We must learn by discernment to separate the evil growth of our actions from the good ground of the soul. And we must prepare that ground so that a new life can grow up from it within us, beyond our knowledge and beyond our conscious control. The sacred attitude is then one of reverence, awe, and silence before the mystery that begins to take place within us when we become aware of our inmost self. In silence, hope, expectation, and unknowing, the man of faith abandons himself to the divine will: not as to an arbitrary and magic power whose decrees must be spelt out from cryptic cyphers, but as to the stream of reality and of life itself. The sacred attitude is then one of deep and fundamental respect for the real in whatever new form it may present itself. The secular attitude is one of gross disrespect for reality, upon which the worldly mind seeks only to force its own crude patterns. The secular man is the slave of his own prejudices, preconceptions and limitations. The man of faith is ideally free from prejudice and plastic in his uninhibited response to each new movement of the stream of life. I say "ideally" in order to exclude those whose faith is not pure but is also another form of prejudice enthroned in the exterior man—a preconceived opinion rather than a living responsiveness to the *logos* of each new situation. For there exists a kind of "hard" and rigid religious faith that is not really alive or spiritual, but resides entirely in the exterior self and is the product of conventionalism and systematic prejudice.   (CQR 215–16)

◆ ◆ ◆

Am I sure that the meaning of my life is the meaning God intends for it? Does God impose a meaning on my life from the *outside,* through event, custom, routine, law, system, impact with others in society? Or am I called to *create from within,* with him, with his grace, a meaning which reflects his truth and makes me his "word" spoken freely in my personal situation? My true identity lies hidden in God's call to my freedom and my response to him. This means I must use my freedom in order to *love,* with full responsibility and authenticity, not merely receiving a form imposed on me by external forces, or forming my own life according to an approved social pattern, but directing my love to the personal reality of my brother, and embracing God's will in its naked, often impenetrable mystery.

(CTP 68)

◆ ◆ ◆

To allow oneself to be carried away by a multitude of conflicting concerns, to surrender to too many demands, to commit oneself to too many projects, to want to help everyone in everything is to succumb to violence. More than that, it is cooperation in violence. The frenzy of the activist neutralizes his work for peace. It destroys his own inner capacity for peace. It destroys the fruitfulness of his own work, because it kills the root of inner wisdom which makes work fruitful. (CGB 73)

◆ ◆ ◆

In moments that appear to be lucid, I tell myself that in times like these there has to be something for which one is willing to get shot, and for which, in all probability, one is actually going to get shot. What is this? A principle? Faith? Virtue? God? The question is not easy to answer and perhaps it has no answer that can be put into words. Perhaps this is no longer something communicable, or even thinkable. To be executed today (and death by execution is not at all uncommon) one has no need to commit a political crime, to express opposition to a tyrant, or even to hold an objectionable opinion. Indeed most political deaths under tyrannical regimes are motiveless, arbitrary, absurd. You are shot, or beaten to death, or starved, or worked until you drop, not because of anything you have done, not because of anything you believe in, not because of anything you stand for, but arbitrarily: your death is demanded by something or someone undefined. Your death is necessary to give apparent meaning to a meaningless political process which you have never quite managed to understand. Your death is necessary to exercise a hypothetical influence on a hypothetical person who might conceivably be opposed to something you may or may not know or understand or like or hate.

Your death is necessary not because you yourself are opposed to anything, or in favor of anything, but simply because people have to keep dying in order to make clear that opposition to those in power is neither practical nor even thinkable. Your death is necessary as a kind of exorcism of the abstract specter of opposition in the minds of leaders whose dishonesty makes them well enough aware that they ought to be opposed. Two thousand years ago the death of a Christian martyr was a supreme affirmation not only of faith, but of liberty. The Christian proved by martyrdom that he had reached a degree of independence in which it no longer mattered to him whether he lived on earth and that it was not necessary for him to save his life by paying official religious homage to the emperor. He was beyond life and death. He had attained to a condition in which all things were "one" and equal to him.   (CGB 91–92)

◆ ◆ ◆

I am more and more impressed by the fact that it is largely futile to get up and make statements about current problems. At the same time, I know that silent acquiescence in evil is also out of the question. I know too that there are times when protest is inescapable, even when it seems as useless as beating your head up against a brick wall. At the same time, when protest simply becomes an act of desperation, it loses its power to communicate anything to anyone who does not share the same feelings of despair.

There is of course no need to comment on the uselessness of false optimism, or to waste any attentions on the sunlit absurdities of those who consistently refuse to face reality. One cannot be a Christian today without having a deeply afflicted conscience. I say it again: we are all under judgment. And it seems to me that our gestures of repentance, though they may be individually sincere, are collectively hollow and even meaningless. Why?

This is the question that plagues me.

The reason seems to be, to some extent, a deep failure of communication.   (FAV 147)

◆ ◆ ◆

If I insist on giving you my truth, and never stop to receive your truth in return, then there can be no truth between us. Christ is present "where two or three are gathered in my name." But to be gathered in the name of Christ is to be gathered in the name of the Word made flesh, of God made man. It is therefore to be gathered in the faith that God has become man and can be seen in man, that he can speak in man and that he can enlighten and inspire love in and through any man I meet. It is true that the visible Church alone has the official mission to sanctify and teach all nations, but no man knows that the stranger he meets coming out of the forest in a new country is not already an invisible member of Christ and perhaps one who has some providential or prophetic message to utter.

(CP 383)

◆ ◆ ◆

Compassion and respect enable us to know the solitude of another by finding him in the intimacy of our own interior solitude. It discovers his secrets in our own secrets. Instead of consuming him with indiscretion, and thus frustrating all our own desires to show our love for him, if we respect the secrecy of his own interior loneliness, we are united with him in a friendship that makes us both grow in likeness to one another and to God. If I respect my brother's solitude, I will know his solitude by the reflection that it casts, through charity, upon the solitude of my own soul.

This respect for the deepest values hidden in another's personality is more than an obligation of charity. It is a debt we owe in justice to every being, but especially to those who, like ourselves, are created in the image of God.

Our failure to respect the intimate spiritual privacy of other persons reflects a secret contempt for God Himself. It springs from the crass pride of fallen man, who wants to prove himself a god by prying into everything that is not his own business.   (NM 245)

◆ ◆ ◆

We do not exist for ourselves alone, and it is only when we are fully convinced of this fact that we begin to love ourselves properly and thus also love others. What do I mean by loving ourselves properly? I mean, first of all, desiring to live, accepting life as a very great gift and a great good, not because of what it gives us, but because of what it enables us to give to others. . . .

If we live for others, we will gradually discover that no one expects us to be "as gods." We will see that we are human, like everyone else, that we all have weaknesses and deficiencies, and that these limitations of ours play a most important part in all our lives. It is because of them that we need others and others need us. We are not all weak in the same spots, and so we supplement and complete one another, each one making up in himself for the lack in another.

(NM xx, xxi)

◆ ◆ ◆

Our task now is to learn that if we can voyage to the ends of the earth and find *ourselves* in the aborigine who most differs from ourselves, we will have made a fruitful pilgrimage. That is why pilgrimage is necessary, in some shape or other. Mere sitting at home and meditating on the divine presence is not enough for our time. We have to come to the end of a long journey and see that the stranger we meet there is no other than ourselves—which is the same as saying we find Christ in him.

For if the Lord is risen, as He said, He is actually or potentially alive in every man. Our pilgrimage to the Holy Sepulchre* is our pilgrimage to the stranger who is Christ our fellow pilgrim and brother. (M&Z 112)

◆ ◆ ◆

If I can unite *in myself* the thought and the devotion of Eastern and Western Christendom, the Greek and the Latin Fathers, the Russians with the Spanish mystics, I can prepare in myself the reunion of divided Christians. From that secret and unspoken unity in myself can eventually come a visible and manifest unity of all Christians. If we want to bring together what is divided, we can not do so by imposing one division upon the other or absorbing one division into the other. But if we do this, the union is not Christian. It is political, and doomed to further conflict. We must contain all divided worlds in ourselves and transcend them in Christ. (CGB 12)

◆ ◆ ◆

Into this world, this demented inn, in which there is absolutely no room for Him at all, Christ has come uninvited. But because He cannot be at home in it, because He is out of place in it, and yet He must be in it, His place is with those others for whom there is no room. His place is with those who do not belong, who are rejected by power because they are regarded as weak, those who are discredited, who are denied the status of persons, tortured, exterminated. With those for whom there is no room, Christ is present in this world. He is mysteriously present in those for whom there seems to be nothing but the world at its worst. For them, there is no escape even in imagination. They cannot identify with the power structure

*Site of the crucifixion, death, burial, and resurrection of Jesus.

of a crowded humanity which seeks to project itself outward, anywhere, in a centrifugal flight into the void, to get *out there* where
there is no God, no man, no name, no identity, no weight, no self,
nothing but the bright, self-directed, perfectly obedient and infinitely expensive machine. (RU 72–73)

◆ ◆ ◆

There is another kind of justice than the justice of number, which
can neither forgive nor be forgiven. There is another kind of mercy
than the mercy of Law which knows no absolution. There is a justice
of newborn worlds which cannot be counted. There is a mercy of
individual things that spring into being without reason. They are
just without reason, and their mercy is without explanation. They
have received rewards beyond description because they themselves
refuse to be described. They are virtuous in the sight of God because their names do not identify them. Every plant that stands in
the light of the sun is a saint and an outlaw. Every tree that brings
forth blossoms without the command of man is powerful in the sight
of God. Every star that man has not counted is a world of sanity
and perfection. Every blade of grass is an angel singing in a shower
of glory.

These are worlds of themselves. No man can use or destroy them.
Theirs is the life that moves without being seen and cannot be understood. It is useless to look for what is everywhere. It is hopeless
to hope for what cannot be gained because you already have it. The
fire of a wild white sun has eaten up the distance between hope and
despair. Dance in this sun, you tepid idiot. Wake up and dance in
the clarity of perfect contradiction. (RU 106–107)

◆ ◆ ◆

It is useless to try to make peace with ourselves by being pleased with everything we have done. In order to settle down in the quiet of our own being we must learn to be detached from the results of our own activity. We must withdraw ourselves, to some extent, from effects that are beyond our control and be content with the good will and the work that are the quiet expression of our inner life. We must be content to live without watching ourselves live, to work without expecting an immediate reward, to love without an instantaneous satisfaction, and to exist without any special recognition.

It is only when we are detached from ourselves that we can be at peace with ourselves. We cannot find happiness in our work if we are always extending ourselves beyond ourselves and beyond the sphere of our work in order to find ourselves greater than we are.

Our Christian destiny is, in fact, a great one: but we cannot achieve greatness unless we lose all interest in being great. For our own idea of greatness is illusory. (NM 121)

♦ ♦ ♦

There is a certain innocence in not having a solution. There is a certain innocence in a kind of despair: but only if in despair we find salvation. I mean, despair of this world and what is in it. Despair of men and of their plans, in order to hope for the impossible answer that lies beyond our earthly contradictions, and yet can burst into our world and solve them only if there are some who hope in spite of despair.

The true solutions are not those which we force upon life in accordance with our theories, but those which life itself provides for those who dispose themselves to receive the truth. Consequently our task is to dissociate ourselves from all who have theories which promise clear and infallible solutions, and to mistrust all such theories not in a spirit of negativism and defeat, but rather trusting life itself, and nature, and if you will permit me, God above all. For since man has decided to occupy the place of God he has shown himself to be far the blindest, and cruelest, and pettiest and most ridiculous of all the false gods. We can call ourselves innocent only if we refuse to forget this, and if we also do everything we can to make others realize it. (RU 60-61)

NONVIOLENCE

Nonviolence is perhaps the most exacting of all forms of struggle, not only because it demands first of all that one be ready to suffer evil and even face the threat of death without violent retaliation, but because it excludes mere transient self-interest from its considerations. In a very real sense, he who practices nonviolent resistance must commit himself not to the defense of his own interests or even those of a particular group: he must commit himself to the defense of objective truth and right and above all of *man*. His aim is then not simply to "prevail" or to prove that he is right and the adversary wrong, or to make the adversary give in and yield what is demanded of him.

Nor should the nonviolent resister be content to prove to *himself* that *he* is virtuous and right, and that *his* hands and heart are pure even though the adversary's may be evil and defiled. Still less should he seek for himself the psychological gratification of upsetting the adversary's conscience and perhaps driving him to an act of bad faith and refusal of the truth. We know that our unconscious motives may, at times, make our nonviolence a form of moral aggression and even a subtle provocation designed (without our awareness) to bring out the evil we hope to find in the adversary, and thus to justify ourselves in our own eyes and in the eyes of "decent people."

(PP 249)

◆ ◆ ◆

Has nonviolence been found wanting? Yes and no. It has been found wanting wherever it has been the nonviolence of the weak. It has not been found wanting when it has been the nonviolence of the strong. What is the difference? It is a difference of language. The language of spurious nonviolence is merely another, more equivocal form of the language of power. It is used and conceived pragmatically, in reference to the seizure of power. But that is not what nonviolence is about. Nonviolence is not for power but for truth. It is not pragmatic but prophetic. It is not aimed at immediate political results, but at the manifestation of fundamental and crucially important truth. Nonviolence is not primarily the language of efficacy, but the language of *kairos.** It does not say "We shall overcome" so much as "This is the day of the Lord, and whatever may happen to us, *He* shall overcome."

(LE 28)

◆ ◆ ◆

There can be no question that unless war is abolished the world will remain constantly in a state of madness and desperation in which, because of the immense destructive power of modern weapons, the danger of catastrophe will be imminent and probably at every moment everywhere. Unless we set ourselves immediately to this task, both as individuals and in our political and religious groups, we

*Kairos is a Greek word that literally means "the fullness of time." It refers to the propitious moment for the performance of an action or the coming into being of a new state; the time of urgent and providential decision.

tend by our passivity and fatalism to cooperate with the destructive forces that are leading inexorably to war. It is a problem of terrifying complexity and magnitude, for which the Church herself is not fully able to see clear and decisive solutions. Yet she must lead the way on the road towards nonviolent settlement of difficulties and towards the gradual abolition of war as the way of settling international or civil disputes. Christians must become active in every possible way, mobilizing all their resources for the fight against war. First of all there is much to be studied, much to be learned. Peace is to be preached, nonviolence is to be explained as a practical method, and not left to be mocked as an outlet for crackpots who want to make a show of themselves. Prayers and sacrifice must be used as the most effective spiritual weapons in the war against war, and like all weapons they must be used with deliberate aim: not just with a vague aspiration for peace and security, but against violence and against war. This implies that we are also willing to sacrifice and restrain our own instinct for violence and aggressiveness in our relations with other people. We may never succeed in this campaign, but whether we succeed or not, the duty is evident. It is the great Christian task of our time. Everything else is secondary, for the survival of the human race itself depends upon it. We must at least face this responsibility and do something about it. And the first job of all is to understand the psychological forces at work in ourselves and in society. (RW 1)

◆　◆　◆

Nonviolence must be aimed above all at the transformation of the present state of the world, and it must therefore be free from all occult, unconscious connivance with an unjust use of power. This poses enormous problems—for if nonviolence is too political it becomes drawn into the power struggle and identified with one side or another in that struggle, while if it is totally apolitical it runs the risk of being ineffective or at best merely symbolic.   (PP 253)

◆ ◆ ◆

It is the refusal of alternatives—a compulsive state of mind which one might call the "ultimatum complex"—which makes wars in order to force the unconditional acceptance of one oversimplified interpretation of reality. This mission of Christian humility in social life is not merely to edify, but to *keep minds open to many alternatives*. The rigidity of a certain type of Christian thought has seriously impaired this capacity, which nonviolence must recover.   (PP 256)

◆ ◆ ◆

Nonviolence seeks to "win" not by destroying or even by humiliating the adversary, but by *convincing him* that there is a higher and more certain common good than can be attained by bombs and blood. Nonviolence, ideally speaking, does not try to overcome the adversary by winning over him, but to turn him from an adversary into a collaborator by winning him over. Unfortunately, non-violent resistance as practiced by those who do not understand it and have not been trained in it, is often only a weak and veiled form of psychological aggression.   (FAV 12–13)

◆ ◆ ◆

*Ahimsa** (nonviolence) is for Gandhi the basic law of our being. That is why it can be used as the most effective principle for social action, since it is in deep accord with the truth of man's nature and

*The Sanskrit word *ahimsa* literally means "without" (*a-*) "injury" (*-himsa*).

corresponds to his innate desire for peace, justice, order, freedom, and personal dignity. Since *himsa* (violence) degrades and corrupts man, to meet force with force and hatred with hatred only increases man's progressive degeneration. Non-violence, on the contrary, heals and restores man's nature, while giving him a means to restore social order and justice. *Ahimsa* is not a policy for the seizure of power. It is a way of transforming relationships so as to bring about a peaceful transfer of power, effected freely and without compulsion by all concerned, because all have come to recognize it as right.

Since *ahimsa* is in man's nature itself, it can be learned by all, though Gandhi is careful to state that he does not expect everyone to practice it perfectly. However, all men should be willing to engage in the risk and wager of *ahimsa* because violent policies have not only proved bankrupt but threaten man with extinction.   (GON 23)

◆　◆　◆

Nonviolence must . . . avoid the ambiguity of an unclear and *confusing protest* that hardens the warmakers in their self-righteous blindness. This means in fact that *in this case above all nonviolence must avoid a facile and fanatical self-righteousness,* and refrain from being satisfied with dramatic self-justifying gestures.

Perhaps the most insidious temptation to be avoided is one which is characteristic of the power structure itself: this fetishism of immediate visible results. Modern society understands "possibilities" and "results" in terms of a superficial and quantitative idea of efficacy. One of the missions of Christian nonviolence is to restore a different standard of practical judgment in social conflicts. This means that the Christian humility of nonviolent action must establish itself in the minds and memories of modern man not only as *conceivable* and *possible,* but as *a desirable alternative* to what he now considers the only realistic possibility: namely, political technique backed by force. Here the human dignity of nonviolence must manifest itself clearly in terms of a freedom and a nobility which are able to resist political manipulation and brute force and show them up as arbitrary, barbarous, and irrational. This will not be easy. The temptation to get publicity and quick results by spectacular tricks or by forms of protest that are merely odd and provocative but whose human meaning is not clear may defeat this purpose.   (PP 253–54)

◆ ◆ ◆

Gandhi does not envisage a tactical non-violence confined to one area of life or to an isolated moment. His non-violence is a creed which embraces all of life in a consistent and logical network of obligations. One cannot be violent, for example, in interpersonal or family relations, and non-violent with regard to conscription and war. Genuine non-violence means not only non-cooperation with glaring social evils, but also the renunciation of benefits and privileges that are implicitly guaranteed by forces which conscience cannot accept.   (GON 51)

◆ ◆ ◆

Strong hate, the hate that takes joy in hating, is strong because it does not believe itself to be unworthy and alone. It feels the support of a justifying God, of an idol of war, an avenging and destroying spirit. From such blood-drinking gods the human race was once liberated, with great toil and terrible sorrow, by the death of a God Who delivered Himself to the Cross and suffered the pathological cruelty of His own creatures out of pity for them. In conquering death He opened their eyes to the reality of a love which asks no questions about worthiness, a love which overcomes hatred and destroys death. But men have now come to reject this divine revelation of pardon, and they are consequently returning to the old war gods, the gods that insatiably drink blood and eat the flesh of men. It is easier to serve the hate-gods because they thrive on the worship of collective fanaticism. To serve the hate-gods, one has only to be blinded by collective passion. To serve the God of Love one must be free, one must face the terrible responsibility of the decision to love *in spite of all unworthiness* whether in oneself or in one's neighbor. (NS 73–74)

◆　◆　◆

The non-violence of the weak is rather a policy of passive protest, or even a cloak for impotent hatred which does not dare to use force. It is without love. It seeks to harm the adversary in ways that do not involve force, and it may resort to secret sabotage or even terrorism. Such conduct is not worthy of the name of non-violence. It is demoralizing and destructive.

To this false and cowardly non-violence Gandhi says he would prefer an honest resort to force. Hence those who cannot practice a really dedicated non-violence should defend their rights and justice by force, if no other means are available. Gandhi does not preach the passive surrender of rights or of human dignity. On the contrary, he believes that nonviolence is the noblest as well as the most effective way of defending one's rights. (GON 35)

◆　◆　◆

Instead of trying to use the adversary as leverage for one's own effort to realize an ideal, nonviolence seeks only to enter into a dialogue with him in order to attain, together with him, the common good of *man.* Nonviolence must be realistic and concrete. Like ordinary political action, it is no more than the "art of the possible." But precisely the advantage of nonviolence is that it has a *more Christian and more humane notion of what is possible.* Where the powerful believe that only power is efficacious, the nonviolent resister is persuaded of the superior efficacy of love, openness, peaceful negotiation, and above all of truth. For power can guarantee the interests of *some men* but it can never foster the good of *man.* Power always protects the good of some at the expense of all the others. Only love can attain and preserve the good of all. Any claim to build the security of *all* on force is a manifest imposture.   (PP 254)

◆   ◆   ◆

A test of our sincerity in the practice of nonviolence is this: are we willing to *learn something from the adversary?* If a *new truth* is made known to us by him or through him, will we accept it? Are we willing to admit that he is not totally inhumane, wrong, unreasonable, cruel, etc.? This is important. If he sees that we are completely incapable of listening to him with an open mind, our nonviolence will have nothing to say to him except that we distrust him and seek to outwit him. Our readiness to see some good in him and to agree with some of his ideas (though tactically this might look like a weakness on our part), actually gives us power: the power of sincerity and of truth. On the other hand, if we are obviously unwilling to accept any truth that we have not first discovered and declared ourselves, we show by that very fact that we are interested not in the truth so much as in "being right." Since the adversary is presumably interested in being right also, and in proving himself right by what he considers the superior argument of force, we end up where we started. Nonviolence has great power, provided that it really witnesses to truth and not just to self-righteousness.

The dread of being open to the ideas of others generally comes from our hidden insecurity about our own convictions. We fear that we may be "converted"—or perverted by a pernicious doctrine. On the other hand, if we are mature and objective in our open-mindedness, we may find that viewing things from a basically different perspective—that of our adversary—we discover our own truth in a new light and are able to understand our own ideal more realistically.

(PP 255)

◆   ◆   ◆

It is therefore very important to understand that Christian humility implies not only a certain wise reserve in regard to one's own judgments—a good sense which sees that we are not always necessarily infallible in our ideas—but it also cherishes positive and trustful expectations of others. A supposed "humility" which is simply depressed about itself and about the world is usually a false humility. This negative, self-pitying "humility" may cling desperately to dark and apocalyptic expectations, and refuse to let go of them. It is secretly convinced that only tragedy and evil can possibly come from our present world situation. This secret conviction cannot be kept hidden. It will manifest itself in our attitudes, in our social action and in our protest. It will show that in fact we despair of reasonable dialogue with anyone. It will show that we expect only the worst. Our action seeks only to block or frustrate the adversary in some way. A protest that from the start declares itself to be in despair is hardly likely to have valuable results. At best it provides an outlet for the personal frustrations of the one protesting. It enables him to articulate his despair in public. This is not the function of Christian nonviolence. This pseudo-prophetic desperation has nothing to do with the beatitudes, even the third.* No blessedness has been promised to those who are merely sorry for themselves.   (PP 256–57)

*The third beatitude is "Blessed are the meek, for they shall inherit the earth"(Matthew 5:5).

◆ ◆ ◆

The meekness and humility which Christ extolled in the Sermon on the Mount and which are the basis of true Christian nonviolence are inseparable from an eschatological Christian hope which is completely open to the presence of God in the world and therefore [to] the presence of our brother who is always seen, no matter who he may be, in the perspectives of the Kingdom. Despair is not permitted to the meek, the humble, the afflicted, the ones famished for justice, the merciful, the clean of heart and the peacemakers. All the beatitudes "hope against hope," "bear everything, believe everything, hope for everything, endure everything" (I Corinthians 13:7). The beatitudes are simply aspects of love. They refuse to despair of the world and abandon it to a supposedly evil fate which it has brought upon itself. Instead, like Christ himself, the Christian takes upon his own shoulders the yoke of the Savior, meek and humble of heart. This yoke is the burden of the world's sin with all its confusions, and all its problems. These sins, confusions and problems are our very own. We do not disown them.   (PP 257)

◆ ◆ ◆

Wherever there is a high moral ideal there is an attendant risk of pharisaism, and nonviolence is no exception. The basis of pharisaism is division: on one hand this morally or socially privileged self and the elite to which it belongs. On the other hand, the "others," the wicked, the unenlightened, whoever they may be, Communists, capitalists, colonialists, traitors, international Jewry, racists, etc.

Christian nonviolence is not built on a presupposed division, but on the basic unity of man. It is not out for the conversion of the wicked to the ideas of the good, but for the healing and reconcilia-

tion of man with himself, man the person, and man the human
family.   (PP 249)

◆ ◆ ◆

It would be a serious mistake to regard Christian non-violence simply as a novel tactic which is at once efficacious and even edifying,
and which enables the sensitive man to participate in the struggles
of the world without being dirtied with blood. Non-violence is not
simply a way of proving one's point and getting what one wants
without being involved in behavior that one considers ugly and evil.
Nor is it, for that matter, a means which anyone can legitimately
make use of according to his fancy for any purpose whatever. To
practice non-violence for a purely selfish or arbitrary end would in
fact discredit and distort the truth of non-violent resistance. To use
non-violence merely in order to gain political advantage at the expense of the opponent's violent mistakes would also be an abuse of
this tactic.   (FAV 14)

◆ ◆ ◆

The nonviolent resister is not fighting simply for "his" truth or for
"his" pure conscience, or for the right that is on "his side." On the
contrary, both his strength and his weakness come from the fact that
he is fighting for *the* truth, common to him and to the adversary, *the*
right which is objective and universal. He is fighting for *everybody*.

For this very reason, as Gandhi saw, the fully consistent practice
of non-violence demands a solid metaphysical and religious basis
both in being and in God. This comes before subjective good intentions and sincerity. For the Hindu this metaphysical basis was pro-

vided by the Vedantist* doctrine of the Atman,† the true transcendent Self which alone is absolutely real, and before which the empirical self of the individual must be effaced in the faithful practice of *dharma*.‡ For the Christian, the basis of non-violence is the Gospel message of salvation for *all* men and of the Kingdom of God to which *all* are summoned. The disciple of Christ, he who has heard the good news, the announcement of the Lord's coming and of His victory, and is aware of the definitive establishment of the Kingdom, proves his faith by the gift of his whole self to the Lord in order that *all* may enter the Kingdom. This Christian discipleship entails a certain way of acting, a *politeia*,§ a *conversatio*,¶ which is proper to the Kingdom.   (FAV 15–16)

◆　◆　◆

Do not be too quick to assume your enemy is a savage just because he is *your* enemy. Perhaps he is your enemy because he thinks you are a savage. Or perhaps he is afraid of you because he feels that you are afraid of him. And perhaps if he believed you were capable of loving him he would no longer be your enemy.

Do not be too quick to assume that your enemy is an enemy of God just because he is *your* enemy. Perhaps he is your enemy pre-

---

*The word *Vedanta* is Sanskrit for "end of the Vedas" where the commentaries, and hence theological concepts, begin.

†*Atman* is Sanskrit for "breath, self, soul, universal self, supreme spirit, the innermost essence of each individual" (*Webster's New International Dictionary,* 3d ed.).

‡*Dharma* is used in both Hinduism and Buddhism to mean, depending on the context, the way, the law, righteousness, reality, one's true life's purpose.

§The Greek word *politeia* means "a way of acting responsibly toward one's community." It is derived from *polis* ("city-state") and *polites* ("citizen").

¶The Latin word *conversatio* refers to a way of acting with perfect charity by means of a monastic manner of life.

cisely because he can find nothing in you that gives glory to God. Perhaps he fears you because he can find nothing in you of God's love and God's kindness and God's patience and mercy and understanding of the weaknesses of men.

Do not be too quick to condemn the man who no longer believes in God, for it is perhaps your own coldness and avarice, your mediocrity and materialism, your sensuality and selfishness that have killed his faith. (NS 177)

◆ ◆ ◆

The hope of the Christian must be, like the hope of a child, pure and full of trust. The child is totally available in the present because he has relatively little to remember, his experience of evil is as yet brief, and his anticipation of the future does not extend far. The Christian, in his humility and faith, must be as totally available to his brother, to his world, in the present, as the child is. But he cannot see the world with childlike innocence and simplicity unless his memory is cleared of past evils by forgiveness, and his anticipation of the future is hopefully free of craft and calculation. For this reason, the humility of Christian nonviolence is at once patient and uncalculating. The chief difference between nonviolence and violence is that the latter depends entirely on its own calculations. The former depends entirely on God and on His word. (PP 257-58)

SAINTHOOD

When Lax* and I were walking down Sixth Avenue, one night in the spring, the street was all torn up and trenched and banked high

---

*"Lax" is Robert Lax, who later converted to Catholicism and became known for his experimental poetry.

with dirt and marked out with red lanterns where they were digging the subway, and we picked our way along the fronts of the dark little stores, going downtown to Greenwich Village. I forget what we were arguing about, but in the end Lax suddenly turned around and asked me the question:

"What do you want to be, anyway?"

I could not say, "I want to be Thomas Merton the well-known writer of all those book reviews in the back pages of the *Times Book Review*," or "Thomas Merton the assistant instructor of Freshman English at the New Life Social Institute for Progress and Culture," so I put the thing on the spiritual plane, where I knew it belonged and said:

"I don't know; I guess what I want is to be a good Catholic."

"What do you mean, you want to be a good Catholic?"

The explanation I gave was lame enough, and expressed my confusion, and betrayed how little I had really thought about it at all.

Lax did not accept it.

"What you should say"—he told me—"what you should say is that you want to be a saint."

A saint! The thought struck me as a little weird. I said:

"How do you expect me to become a saint?"

"By wanting to," said Lax, simply.

"I can't be a saint," I said, "I can't be a saint." And my mind darkened with a confusion of realities and unrealities: the knowledge of my own sins, and the false humility which makes men say that they cannot do the things that they *must* do, cannot reach the level that they *must* reach: the cowardice that says: "I am satisfied to save my soul, to keep out of mortal sin," but which means, by those words: "I do not want to give up my sins and my attachments."

But Lax said: "No. All that is necessary to be a saint is to want to be one. Don't you believe that God will make you what He created you to be, if you will consent to let Him do it? All you have to do is desire it." (SSM 237-38)

◆ ◆ ◆

I wonder if there are twenty men alive in the world now who see things as they really are. That would mean that there were twenty men who were free, who were not dominated or even influenced by any attachment to any created thing or to their own selves or to any gift of God, even to the highest, the most supernaturally pure of His graces. I don't believe that there are twenty such men alive in the world. But there must be one or two. They are the ones who are holding everything together and keeping the universe from falling apart. (NS 203)

◆ ◆ ◆

In the collapse of medieval society, amid the corruption of the clergy and the decadence of conventional life, there arose men and women of the laity who were *perfectly obedient to God*. Nicholas of Flue, for instance, and Joan of Arc. They were simple and straightforward signs of contradiction in the middle of worldliness, prejudice, cruelty, despair, and greed. They were *not rebels* at all. They were meek and submissive instruments of God who, while being completely opposed to the corrupt norms around them, gave every man and every authority his due. They show clearly and convincingly what it is to be not a rebel, but obedient to God as a sign to men—a sign of mercy, a revelation of truth and power. We are spontaneously drawn to these signs of God with all the love of our hearts. We naturally trust them, believe in their intercession, knowing that they live in the glory of God and that God would not give us such love for them if they were not still "sacraments" of His mercy to us. (CGB 145)

◆ ◆ ◆

We tend to think of "the martyrs" as men of a different stamp from ourselves, men of another age, bred in another atmosphere, men somehow stronger and greater than we. But it turns out that we too are expected to face the same sufferings and confess Christ and die for Him. We who are not heroes are the ones God is choosing to share the lot of His great warriors. And one look into our own souls tells us that there is nothing there that invites the combats of the mighty saints. There is nothing magnificent about us. We are miserable things and if we are called upon to die we shall die miserably. There is nothing of grandeur about us. We are null. And perhaps we are already marked for sacrifice—a sacrifice that will be, in the eyes of the world, perhaps only drab and sorry and mean. And yet it will end by being our greatest glory after all. Perhaps there is no greater glory than to be reduced to insignificance by an unjust and stupid temporal power, in order that God may triumph over evil through our insignificance. (soj 79)

◆　◆　◆

Some men have been picked out to bear witness to Christ's love in lives overwhelmed by suffering. These have proclaimed that suffering was their vocation. But that should not lead us to believe that in order to be a saint one must go out for suffering in the same way that a college athlete goes out for football. No two men have to suffer exactly the same trials in exactly the same way. No one man is ever called to suffer merely for the sake of suffering. (nm 80)

◆　◆　◆

The saint is not one who accepts suffering because he likes it, and confesses this preference before God and men in order to win a great reward. He is one who may well hate suffering as much as anybody else, but who so loves Christ, Whom he does not see, that he will allow His love to be proved by any suffering. And he does this not because he thinks it is an achievement, but because the charity of Christ in his heart demands that it be done. (NM 79–80)

◆ ◆ ◆

The saint, therefore, is sanctified not only by fasting when he should fast but also by eating when he should eat. He is not only sanctified by his prayers in the darkness of the night, but by the sleep that he takes in obedience to God, Who made us what we are. Not only His solitude contributes to his union with God, but also his supernatural love for his friends and his relatives and those with whom he lives and works.   (NM 99)

◆ ◆ ◆

One of the first signs of a saint may well be the fact that other people do not know what to make of him. In fact, they are not sure whether he is crazy or only proud; but it must at least be pride to be haunted by some individual ideal which nobody but God really comprehends. And he has inescapable difficulties in applying all the abstract norms of "perfection" to his own life. He cannot seem to make his life fit in with the books.

Sometimes his case is so bad that no monastery will keep him. He has to be dismissed, sent back to the world like Benedict Joseph Labre, who wanted to be a Trappist and a Carthusian and succeeded in neither. He finally ended up as a tramp. He died in some street in Rome.

And yet the only canonized saint, venerated by the whole Church, who has lived either as a Cistercian or a Carthusian since the Middle Ages is St. Benedict Joseph Labre.   (NS 103)

◆　◆　◆

The saints are what they are, not because their sanctity makes them admirable to others, but *because the gift of sainthood makes it possible for them to admire everybody else.*   (NS 57)

◆　◆　◆

For me to be a saint means to be myself. Therefore the problem of sanctity and salvation is in fact the problem of finding out who I am and of discovering my true self.

Trees and animals have no problem. God makes them what they are without consulting them, and they are perfectly satisfied.

With us it is different. God leaves us free to be whatever we like. We can be ourselves or not, as we please. We are at liberty to be real, or to be unreal. We may be true or false, the choice is ours. We may wear now one mask and now another, and never, if we so desire, appear with our own true face. But we cannot make these choices with impunity. Causes have effects, and if we lie to ourselves and to others, then we cannot expect to find truth and reality whenever we happen to want them. If we have chosen the way of falsity we must not be surprised that truth eludes us when we finally come to need it!   (NS 31–32)

◆　◆　◆

Be content that you are not yet a saint, even though you realize that the only thing worth living for is sanctity. Then you will be satisfied to let God lead you to sanctity by paths that you cannot understand. You will travel in darkness in which you will no longer be concerned with yourself and no longer compare yourself to other men. Those who have gone by that way have finally found out that sanctity is in everything and that God is all around them. Having given up all desire to compete with other men, they suddenly wake up and find that the joy of God is everywhere, and they are able to exult in the virtues and goodness of others more than ever they could have done in their own. They are so dazzled by the reflection of God in the souls of the men they live with that they no longer have any power to condemn anything they see in another. Even in the greatest sinners they can see virtues and goodness that no one else can find. As for themselves, if they still consider themselves, they no longer dare to compare themselves with others. The idea has now become unthinkable. But it is no longer a source of suffering and lamentation: they have finally reached the point where they take their own insignificance for granted. They are no longer interested in their external selves.   (NS 59–60)

Books and Tapes by and about Thomas Merton

Films and Recordings

Merton: A Film Biography of Thomas Merton. Produced by Paul Wilkes. New York: First Run Features (1984). This documentary features the only film ever shot of Thomas Merton and includes interviews with Merton's closest friends and colleagues. Available on video through Amazon.com and other retail outlets.

Lectures by Thomas Merton. 19 cassettes (one hour each). Kansas City, Mo.: Credence Cassettes, 1988, 1990. These are recordings of lectures Merton gave as Novice Master at Gethsemani. Topics range from literary analyses of Rainer Maria Rilke and William Faulkner to discussions of monastic prayer and communism. Not all of the recorded material in the Merton archives has been transferred onto cassettes yet; more tapes may be available in the future.

Other Books by Thomas Merton

This list includes anthologies not mentioned in the works cited but that may be of interest to readers discovering Thomas Merton.

The Hidden Ground of Love: The Letters of Thomas Merton on Religious Experience and Social Concerns. Edited by William H. Shannon. New York: Farrar, Straus, 1985. Altered the face of Merton scholarship by documenting the full extent of his dialogues with thinkers of different backgrounds and traditions.

Loving and Living. Edited by Naomi Burton Stone and Brother Patrick Hart. New York: Farrar, Straus, 1980. Some of Merton's best essays collected by two of his closest colleagues.

Thomas Merton: Essential Writings. Edited by Christine Bochen. Maryknoll, N. Y.: Orbis Books, 2000. This inclusive collection of essays and excerpts covers the entire sweep of Merton's lifework.

A Thomas Merton Reader. Edited by Thomas McDonnell. Garden City, N.Y.: Doubleday, 1974. Merton proofread the copy and helped select the material for this anthology.

Thomas Merton: Spiritual Master. Edited and with an introduction by Lawrence S. Cunningham. New York: Paulist Press, 1992. Contains substantial selections from Merton's most important spiritual writings along with an encyclopedic introductory essay by Professor Cunningham, a chronology of Merton's life, and an extensive bibliography.

Books about Thomas Merton

Dozens of books have been written about Merton, and more come out every year. Listed below are works of particular interest to readers of this volume.

Forest, James. *Thomas Merton: A Pictorial Biography*. New York: Paulist Press, 1980. The story of Merton's life told by a personal friend and member of the Catholic Worker community.

Furlong, Monica. *Merton: A Biography*. San Francisco: Harper and Row, 1981. A succinct analysis of the key issues in Merton's life.

Griffin, John Howard. *The Hermitage Journals*. Garden City, N.Y.: Doubleday Image, 1983. This was the first installment of Griffin's inspired but never completed authorized biography of Thomas Merton. Griffin, famous author of *Black Like Me* (1961), died before he could complete his projected multivolume work. Michael Mott took over the project.

Inchausti, Robert. *Thomas Merton's American Prophecy*. Albany: SUNY Press, 1998. This critical biography by the editor of this volume explores Merton's place in American intellectual history.

Mott, Michael. *The Seven Mountains of Thomas Merton*. Boston: Houghton Muffin, 1984. This authorized biography remains the definitive source for the specifics of Merton's life.

Padovano, Anthony. *The Human Journey: Thomas Merton: Symbol of a Century*. Garden City, N.Y.: Doubleday, 1982. Examines Merton's significance as a spiritual master.

Rice, Edward. *The Man in the Sycamore Tree*. Garden City, N.Y.: Doubleday, 1970. Written as a personal tribute to Merton by one of his best friends at Columbia. Currently out of print, this book contains rare photos of Merton and his friends along with reproductions of his sketches first published in the *Columbia Jester*.

Shannon, William H. *Something of a Rebel: Thomas Merton, His Life and Works: An Introduction.* Cincinnati: St. Anthony Messenger Press, 1997. This overview of Merton's life and work, written by one of the world's top Merton scholars, is specifically designed to introduce Merton to new readers.

Wilkes, Paul, ed. *Merton: By Those Who Knew Him Best.* San Francisco: Harper and Row, 1984. A collection of short essays and interviews with Merton's friends and colleagues assessing his life and contribution.

Sources and Abbreviations

AJ   *The Asian Journal of Thomas Merton,* edited by Naomi Burton, Brother Patrick Hart, and James Laughlin (New York: New Directions, 1973).

ATT *The Ascent to Truth* (London: Hollis and Carter, 1951).

BIW *Bread in the Wilderness* (New York: New Directions, 1960).

CFT *The Courage for Truth: The Letters of Thomas Merton to Writers,* selected and edited by Christine M. Bochen (New York: Farrar, Straus & Giroux, 1993).

CGB *Conjectures of a Guilty Bystander* (Garden City, N.Y.: Doubleday, 1966).

CIWA *Contemplation in a World of Action* (Garden City, N.Y.: Doubleday, 1971).

CNP *Centering Prayer,* by Basil Pennington (Garden City, N.Y.: Doubleday, 1982).

CP   *The Collected Poems of Thomas Merton* (New York: New Directions, 1977).

CQR *Cistercian Quarterly Review #18* (1983).

CTP *Contemplative Prayer* (Garden City, N.Y.: Doubleday, 1971).

DQ   *Disputed Questions* (San Diego: Harcourt Brace Jovanovich, 1985).

FAV *Faith and Violence* (Notre Dame, Ind.: University of Notre Dame Press, 1968).

GON *Gandhi on Non-Violence: Selected Texts from Mohandas K. Gandhi's "Non-Violence in Peace and War,"* edited and with an introduction by Thomas Merton (New York: New Directions, 1965).

HGL *The Hidden Ground of Love: Letters on Religious Experience and Social Concerns,* edited by William H. Shannon (New York: Harcourt Brace Jovanovich, 1985).

HR   *"Honorable Reader": Reflections on My Work,* edited by Robert E. Daggy (New York: Crossroad, 1991).

IM   *The Intimate Merton: His Life from His Journals,* edited by Patrick Hart and Jonathan Montaldo (San Francisco: HarperSanFrancisco, 1999).

LE   *The Literary Essays of Thomas Merton,* edited by Patrick Hart (New York: New Directions, 1981).

LL   *Love and Living,* edited by Naomi Burton Stone and Brother Patrick Hart (New York: Farrar, Straus & Giroux, 1980).

MA   *My Argument with the Gestapo* (Garden City, N.Y.: Doubleday, 1969).

MJ   *The Monastic Journey,* edited by Brother Patrick Hart (Kansas City: Sheed, Andrews, 1978).

M&Z   *Mystics and Zen Masters* (New York: Farrar, Straus & Giroux, 1967).

NM   *No Man Is an Island* (New York: Harcourt Brace Jovanovich, 1983).

NS   *New Seeds of Contemplation* (New York: New Directions, 1972).

OTB   *Opening the Bible* (Collegeville, Minn: Liturgical Press 1970).

PP   *Passion for Peace: The Social Essays,* edited by William H. Shannon (New York: Crossroad Press, 1995).

RU   *Raids on the Unspeakable* (New York, New Directions, 1966).

RW   "The Root of War," in *The Catholic Worker* #28, Oct. 1961.

SD&M   *Spiritual Direction and Meditation* (Wheathampstead-Hertfordshire: Anthony Clarke, 1987).

SJ   *The Secular Journal of Thomas Merton* (New York: Farrar, Straus & Cudahy, 1959).

SOJ   *The Sign of Jonas* (San Diego: Harcourt Brace Jovanovich, 1979).

SSM   *The Seven Storey Mountain* (San Diego: Harcourt Brace Jovanovich, 1976).

TIS   *Thoughts in Solitude* (New York: Farrar, Straus, 1958).

WOC   *The Way of Chuang Tzu* (New York: New Directions, 1965).

WOD   *The Wisdom of the Desert* (New York: New Directions, 1960).

Z&B   *Zen and the Birds of Appetite* (New York, New Directions, 1968).

Acknowledgments

Grateful acknowledgment is made to the following publishers for permission to reprint from copyrighted material:

Cistercian Publications for selections from *The Climate of Monastic Prayer* (Kalamazoo, Mich.: Cistercian Publications, 1971), also published as *Contemplative Prayer.*

Cistercian Studies Quarterly for selections from "The Inner Experience" by Thomas Merton. *Cistercian Studies Quarterly*, vols. 17 and 19, copyright by the Trustees of the Merton Legacy Trust.

Crossroad Publishing Company for *Passion for Peace: The Social Essays*, by Thomas Merton, edited by William H. Shannon (New York: Crossroad Press, 1995), copyright by the Trustees of the Merton Legacy Trust.

Doubleday, a division of Random House, for selections from *Centering Prayer* by M. Basil Pennington, copyright 1980 by the Cistercian Abbey of Spencer, Inc.; *Conjectures of a Guilty Bystander,* by Thomas Merton (Garden City, N.Y.: Doubleday, 1966), copyright by the Abbey of Our Lady of Gethsemani; *My Argument with the Gestapo,* by Thomas Merton (Garden City, N.Y.: Doubleday, 1969), copyright by the Abbey of Our Lady of Gethsemani.

Harcourt, Inc., for selections from *The Seven Storey Mountain,* by Thomas Merton (New York: Harcourt Brace Jovanovich, 1948), copyright renewed 1976 by the Trustees of the Merton Legacy Trust; *The Ascent to Truth,* by Thomas Merton (New York: Harcourt Brace Jovanovich, 1951), copyright by the Abbey of Our Lady of Gethsemani; *No Man Is an Island,* by Thomas Merton (New York: Harcourt

Brace Jovanovich, 1955), copyright by the Abbey of Our Lady of Gethsemani and renewed 1976 by the Trustees of the Merton Legacy Trust; *The Sign of Jonas*, by Thomas Merton (New York: Harcourt Brace Jovanovich, 1953), copyright by the Abbey of Our Lady of Gethsemani, renewed 1981 by the Trustees of the Merton Legacy Trust.

New Directions Publishing Corp. for selections from *Bread in the Wilderness,* by Thomas Merton (New York: New Directions, 1953), copyright by the Abbey of Our Lady of Gethsemani; *The Wisdom of the Desert,* by Thomas Merton (New York: New Directions, 1960), copyright by the Abbey of Our Lady of Gethsemani; *The Way of Chuang Tzu* (New York: New Directions, 1965), copyright by the Abbey of Our Lady of Gethsemani; *Raids on the Unspeakable,* by Thomas Merton (New York: New Directions, 1966), copyright by the Abbey of Our Lady of Gethsemani; *Zen and the Birds of Appetite,* by Thomas Merton (New York: New Directions, 1968), copyright by the Abbey of Our Lady of Gethsemani; *The Asian Journal,* by Thomas Merton, ed. Naomi Burton, Brother Patrick Hart, and James Laughlin (New York: New Directions, 1975), copyright by the Trustees of Merton Legacy Trust; *The Collected Poems of Thomas Merton,* by Thomas Merton (New York: New Directions, 1963), copyright by the Abbey of Our Lady of Gethsemani; *New Seeds of Contemplation* by Thomas Merton (New York: New Directions, 1961), copyright by the Abbey of Our Lady of Gethsemani; *The Literary Essays of Thomas Merton,* by Thomas Merton, edited by Patrick Hart (New York: New Directions, 1981), copyright 1960, 1966, 1967, 1968, 1973, 1975, 1978, 1981 by the Trustees of Merton Legacy Trust; copyright 1959, 1961, 1963, 1964, 1965, 1981 by the Abbey of Our Lady of Gethsemani; copyright 1953 by Our Lady of Gethsemani Monastery. *Gandhi on Non-Violence* (New York: New Directions) copyright 1964, 1965.

University of Notre Dame Press for selections from *Contemplation in a World of Action,* by Thomas Merton, copyright 1998 by the University of Notre Dame Press; *Faith and Violence* by Thomas Merton (Notre Dame, Ind.: University of Notre Dame Press, 1984), copyright 1984 by the University of Notre Dame Press.

The Liturgical Press for selections from *Opening the Bible,* by Thomas Merton (Collegeville, Minn.: Liturgical Press, 1970), copyright 1986 by The Order of St. Benedict, Inc.

Sheed and Ward for selections from *The Monastic Journey,* edited by Brother Patrick Hart (Kansas City, Mo.: Sheed, Andrews 1978).

HarperSanFrancisco for a selection from *The Intimate Merton: His Life from His Journals,* edited by Patrick Hart and Jonathan Montaldo (San Francisco: HarperSanFrancisco, 1999), copyright by the Merton Legacy Trust.

The Merton Legacy Trust for a selection from *"Honorable Reader:" Reflections on My Work* by Thomas Merton, edited by Robert Daggy (New York: Crossroad, 1991).